So
Nutrition

Dorothy Lennon
Paul Fieldhouse

FORBES PUBLICATIONS

fp

Dedication

To E.C.W., Zoe and Sophie

Acknowledgements

We are very grateful to the Library staff of Leeds Polytechnic for their help and to Elaine Picker for typing

©Forbes Publications Limited
Redan House, Redan Place,
London W2 4SB

Printed and bound in Great Britain
by Billing and Sons Limited
London and Worcester

Contents

List of tables and figures

SECTION I
Nutrition and health

I: Nutrition as a determinant of health

Over the past two hundred years patterns of illness in Britain have shown considerable change. Improvements in health care are reflected in increased survival rates, as illustrated in *Table 1.1*. Although data on non-fatal illness is either non-existent or else very difficult to assess, it is likely that a similar decline has taken place. Reduction in morbidity and mortality has been largely due to the control of infectious disease associated with advances in public health, such as improved sanitation and specific medical measures, such as immunisation.

Improvements in food supply, preparation and distribution have helped to eradicate many of the nutritional problems formerly seen in Britain. Advances in nutritional knowledge during the early part of the twentieth century led to better recognition of the links between nutrition and ill-health.[1] Government policies implemented during the 1930s and 1940s led to the widespread use of welfare foods and supplements, the introduction of formal school milk and meals schemes and of various fortification measures. The strict control on food supply and availability during the Second World War actually helped to improve the nutritional health of the population. 'The national provision of milk and vitamin supplements has probably done more than any other factor to promote the health of expectant mothers and young children'[2]. But whilst risk of deficiency diseases has been drastically reduced, a different type of malnutrition is now emerging. This may be identified as 'over-nutrition' and has been linked to many of the degenerative diseases common in the modern Western World. Despite the effort of traditional curative

[1] Drummond J.C. and Wilbraham A. (1939) *The Englishman's Food* Jonathan Cape.
[2] Chief Medical Officer, Ministry of Health (1946) *State of the Public Health During Six Years of War* HMSO London.

medicine, the prevalence of these disorders appears to be increasing. Because these disorders – which include obesity, dental disease, diabetes, coronary heart disease and bowel disorders – are thought to be a consequence of changes in lifestyle, they are often referred to as 'diseases of modern civilisation'. Epidemiological evidence suggests that these diseases are far less common, and sometimes unknown, in developing countries: it further indicates that diet may be a major factor responsible for the difference seen. The role of the various dietary factors in relation to health disease is considered in chapter 3.

Health depends on the interplay of a number of complex factors which exert their influence on the lifestyle of the individual. Some of them are beyond the control of the individual, whilst others are more amenable to personal manipulation. Four major interrelated determinants can be identified:

1. Genetics
2. Health services
3. Environment
4. Personal health behaviour

Figure 1.1 illustrates these, and indicates some examples of interrelationships.

Genetics

The first of the determinants to be considered is perhaps the most fundamental one, and it operates in several ways.

Certain individuals are born with specific genetic abnormalities which give rise to particular nutritional problems. The group of disorders known as inborn errors of metabolism are examples of this. Due to a deficiency of a particular enzyme, the body is unable to cope with a normal diet, and dietary manipulations become essential. Phenylketonuria is one of the better known examples of this. Milk intolerance is a not uncommon state in infants, where again, fundamental alterations of diet are needed. Whole population groups can be susceptible to

Table 1.1	Survival rates
Date	50% of population survived to: Age (yr)
1693	10
1850	40
1900	50
1920	60
1970	70

(Figures from *English life tables*)

Adapted from McKeown T., Lowe C.R. (1974) *An introduction to social medicine* Blackwell Oxford. p4.

Figure 1.1 Determinants of health

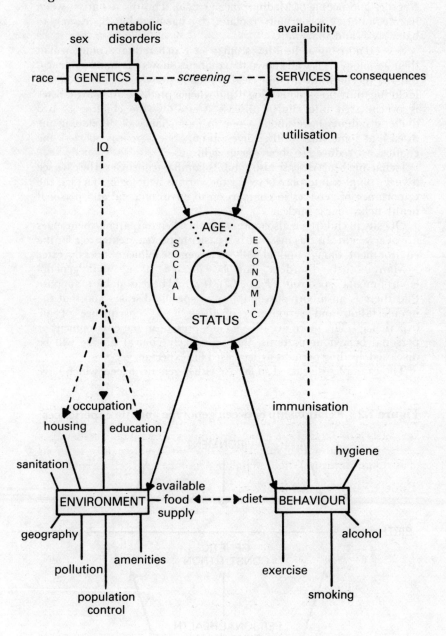

certain disorders, eg sickle cell anaemia, which affects particularly Negroes and people of Mediterranean origin. This disease arises when haemoglobin A is partially replaced by haemoglobin S, leading to haemolysis and anaemia.

Several nutritional disorders seem to have an hereditary component in their aetiology. It is well known that diabetes shows a familial tendency, but the mechanisms are not clear. Probably, environmental factors – including nutrition – determine if and when a predisposition to diabetes is precipitated into clinical disease. Certainly, the children of two diabetic parents have about a one in four chance of developing the disease at some stage of their lives. If only one parent is affected, the chances are reduced to about one in eight.

Ischaemic heart disease also exhibits familial tendencies. Here we see a very complex interplay between the various aetiological factors; the importance of genetics in comparison to environmental and personal health behaviour is unclear.

Obesity in children is also more common when the parents themselves are overweight. In this instance it is easier to posit a greater role for the environment, though undoubtedly some genetic influence does operate.

Many other disorders can be located along the 'genetic-environmental' spectrum. (*Figure 1.2*). It would be reasonable to suppose that there is an inborn susceptibility to specific diseases and that the manifestation and seriousness of these is a consequence of life experiences. The more negative factors present in the environment or personal behaviour patterns, the more likely clinical disease will be disclosed, leading perhaps to decreased life expectancy.

The examples discussed so far are either genetic defects which have

Figure 1.2   Relationship between genotype and life experiences

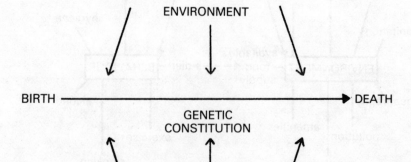

nutritional consequences or nutritional disorders in which there is some inherited trait. A more fundamental effect of genetics is its determination of sex. The disease experiences of the sexes are different, and this can be seen in nutritional disorders. Thus coronary heart disease is much more common in men (and post menopausal women), whilst iron deficiency anaemia is largely confined to women of child bearing age.

It is obvious from the above discussion that the nutritionist must be aware of the part genetics plays in disease causation. At one time it would have been true to say that of the four health determinants initially mentioned, genetics was the only one not susceptible to change. With advances in modern medicine and the advent of genetic counselling, this is no longer strictly true, though it must always remain the least amenable to alteration on both technical and moral grounds.

Services

Provision of health services will affect health status. For example, if no dietetic service is available, then people are less able to seek help with nutritional problems, and it is likely that such untreated conditions as obesity will become more common. The nature of services – whether preventive or curative – is also important: in the case of obesity it becomes progressively more difficult to treat the condition, the longer it has been established. Long term success with reducing diets is notoriously low, and primary prevention would seem to offer a more effective strategy. One of the problems of services is that they are often underutilised by the people who would benefit from them most. Basing services in the community rather than in the hospital may help to make them more accessible and therefore encourage increased utilisation. One example of this is the provision of evening clinics for the benefit of working mothers. The effectiveness of services is important in that user-expectation must be met if high levels of utilisation are to be maintained.

Environment

Both the physical and social environment are important in their effects on health. Environmental improvements leading to better health have already been cited, and a large proportion of the decline in mortality and morbidity of the past century and a half may be attributed to these improvements. In some instances environmental influences have been directly or indirectly detrimental to nutritional status.

An example of this latter occurrence was described by McGonigle and Kirkby (1936).[3] When families from a slum area of Stockton-on-Tees were rehoused in a new housing estate, there followed an increase in

[3]McGonigle and Kirkby (1936) *Poverty and Public Health* Gollancz, London.

mortality rate. Higher rents in the new houses caused a reduction in the amount of money available to purchase food.

In the case of nutrition, the environment provides a framework within which individual choice can operate.

However, **personal health behaviour** is the ultimate arbiter of choice. Individuals will choose what to eat and what not to eat. Similarly, they will choose whether to smoke or drink, whether to take exercise or be immunised, and so on.

The anti-health effects of personal behaviour can be seen to be manifested as:

1) adoption of habits incommensurate with health

2) rejection of health care and non-compliance

3) indirectly, as creation of a high-risk environment

It is because inappropriate behaviour can lead to health problems, that much health education is directed at persuading people to act in their own best interests.

Figure 1.1 indicates that socio-economic status is an important consideration in health, whether a cause or consequence it is inextricably linked to the determinants previously mentioned. Poor mental capability may lead to reduced progress in education and subsequently restrict job opportunities and housing expectation. Lower incomes in turn will restrict food choice. Lack of education may affect personal decision-making skills and contribute to under-use of services, and vulnerability to advertising and commercial pressures. The relative effectiveness of tackling each of the areas described could be endlessly debated. Would we do better to attempt control of environment and services or should we concentrate on influencing personal behaviour? This raises ethical questions and involves value judgements, but it is clear that there are several ways in which the health of the population could be manipulated.

2: Nutritional surveillance

The nutritional status of a population is influenced by a variety of factors. The manifestations of subnutrition and malnutrition vary in type and degree from country to country through differences in food availability and consumption patterns. A population may survive for some time on a marginally inadequate diet, but may be more prone to disease and less efficient both physically and mentally.

Food consumption is influenced by a wide variety of factors, many of which will be discussed in later chapters.

Nutritional surveillance could be said to describe the process of attempting to estimate the number of individuals in a population who are either suffering from, or at risk from, inadequate nutrition. It should further be concerned with identifying the reasons for any malnutrition which may be discovered, and which individuals in a society are most vulnerable to its effects. Corrective or preventive measures can then be determined and steps taken to implement suitable programmes.

Studies may be threefold in nature:

Cross sectional – where detailed information on population samples, as nationally representative as possible, is obtained.

Longitudinal – this can be carried out either by surveying the same individuals over a period of time, or by the use of running indices – for example those used by the DHSS are birth weights, infant mortality and growth rate of school children. Obviously all are affected by other factors, but they can give an indication that more information is needed.

Special studies – these are usually instigated when information on a particular group is needed to elucidate some previous finding.

Different countries have various methods of carrying out nutritional surveillance, which involve a range of governmental and non-governmental agencies. In the United Kingdom, nutritional surveillance has been implemented in a number of ways. Government departments – notably the Department of Health and Social Security – have been responsible for a large number of nutrition surveys. Other work has been carried out by researchers in medical schools and educational institutions, often under the auspices of the Medical Research Council.

The Rothschild Report suggested that the DHSS should sponsor outside research workers to look at problems concerned with nutrition, and not be itself directly involved, other than in a funding capacity.

In Czechoslovakia, the Institute of Human Nutrition was founded in the 1950s and in its early years carried out dietary surveys, and took both clinical and biochemical measurements as well as gathering economic information on large population groups. The Institute carries out any survey necessary, for example, at present it is monitoring the fat intake of the population since this has remained high despite the efforts of health educationalists. Perhaps the most interesting feature of the influence that the Institute exerts is that the results of the earlier dietary surveys were used to elaborate the recommended dietary allowances for Czechoslovakia. The work of the Institute is considered valuable by the Government and is used in preventive medicine, and is considered when decisions are made regarding policy on agriculture and food processing.

The United States of America has various sources of information available about food consumption.

The United States Department of Agriculture's National Nutrient and Food Consumption surveys are carried out at ten year intervals. They have, until the 1965 survey, only collected household food disappearance data, but in the 1965 survey individual food and nutrient intakes using the 24 hour recall method were obtained. These surveys show trends in consumption of food and nutrients and changing dietary patterns, rather than giving detailed information about any other aspects of nutrition such as distribution within the family.

An attempt to evaluate the nutritional status of low income groups throughout the United States was undertaken by the Centre for Disease Control 1968-70. The survey known as the Ten States Survey, included a medical history, physical examination, anthropometric and biochemical measurements as well as a dietary survey. The results obtained are used in America to predict current and future developments in food consumption.

Assessment of nutritional status

There are various methods of assessing nutritional status, and as each one has its limitations, it is therefore better to use more than one method so that more comprehensive information is obtained.

The four main methods of assessing nutritional status are: 1) Dietary, 2) Biochemical, 3) Clinical, 4) Anthropometric.

Dietary

Although dietary studies have various inherent problems, which we shall discuss later, they are still the best method of getting specific information about nutritional status. They not only tell the researcher what food is being eaten but also who gets what within the family and society and hopefully why. They (the dietary surveys) ought to provide the answers to questions such as, is it the price of a food which determines whether it is eaten, or is it unacceptable because of social customs? Food wastage may be ascertained, including how much is given to pets. Once this information is obtained not only can deficiencies in the diet be shown, but acceptable means of improving the diet and making best use of food supplies can be instituted.

METHODS

There are three methods of surveying dietary intake; recall, weighed intake, food purchases. The latter, which is used by the Ministry of Agriculture, Fisheries & Food for their Household Food Consumption surveys, is only useful for showing trends in food consumption and changing dietary patterns.

The choice between recall and a weighed dietary intake needs to be made according to the type of subjects to be involved in the survey and what field workers are available.

In order to carry out a weighed dietary study, subjects must be capable of using scales and recording their food intake, this may seem an obvious consideration but many researchers forget what is commonplace to them will not be to those members of the population they wish to survey. Also the thought of doing a weighed intake for a period of a week, may cause a drop in the recruitment rate.

Recall may be the best method of obtaining the relevant information from certain groups, particuarly those where there is a high rate of illiteracy, or physical handicap prevents the subjects of the survey from writing. It is in using recall for obtaining dietary information that the skill of the field worker is invaluable. The ability to prompt without leading is an essential quality in the researcher and often cross checks can be made using shopping lists. A halfway measure which can be used in dietary surveys is to ask subjects to write down their food intake in a diet diary in household amounts. The researcher can then check the diary with the participant and obtain any more information necessary.

Both methods rely on the fieldworker establishing a rapport with the subject so that mutual trust is built up and the intake recorded is truly reflective of the subject's normal intake.

Dietary surveys must be carried out so that seasonal variations are accounted for, especially where nutrients such as vitamin C are concerned.

Before any survey can be undertaken however, a decision must be taken as to which food analysis tables are suitable, or if none can be found, how food samples are to be analysed; however taking aliquots of food is a much more suitable method for a survey involving an institution where the researcher may be more interested in vitamin losses during food preparation.

So far we have only discussed obtaining information about actual food intake, and as mentioned previously other information is necessary so that acceptable means of improving nutrition can be instituted. The type of information sought may vary according to the group surveyed, but in

9

general some information about economic status, marital status, religion, and housing is invaluable. Obtaining this information means that the interviewer must be able to elicit it without prejudicing the survey's success, ie if the subjects feel that an intrusion into their privacy is being made then they may refuse to continue the survey. Questionnaires need to be drawn up carefully with the advice of sociologists, otherwise the information sought may not be obtained.

Biochemical

Biochemical studies are of course an interesting and useful back up to dietary studies, but can sometimes reflect current or recent nutrition rather than long term. There is a series of events thought to lead to overt deficiency diseases. First there is a depletion of the body nutrient stores, this is usually accompanied by changes in the blood concentration of that nutrient and by a reduced urinary excretion of the nutrient and/or its metabolites. Functional impairment occurs as the deficiency progresses, and in the final stages, the clinical features of the actual deficiency disease are seen.

There are various points in this sequence of events where deficiency of a nutrient could be detected, but the researcher must always bear in mind that any pathological finding may be due to secondary causes such as malabsorption. Results may be misleading for some nutrients; for example, Keys et al found only a slight decrease in the plasma proteins of 34 men maintained on a famine diet for six months.[1]

Different races can show different levels of certain substances, so that what may be considered indicative of deficiency in one race, may be within the normal range for another, eg Negroes have a lower serum albumin and higher globulin level than Europeans.

Clinical methods

The use of clinical signs of deficiency diseases as a method of assessing nutritional status is of debatable value. Firstly the medical researchers should ideally all have the same criteria and diagnostic skill; and secondly signs must be specific for a certain deficiency. For example in the survey conducted on the elderly by the DHSS 1967/68, 57 out of 778 subjects were diagnosed as having angular stomatitis, but their average daily intake of riboflavin was 1.2 mg compared with 1.3 mg for those not showing the condition. This suggests that much of the angular stomatitis was non-nutritional.

[1]Keys A., Taylor, H.L., Michelson O., Henschel A. (1964) *Science* 103, 669.
[2]DHSS (1972) *Nutrition Survey of the Elderly* Report by Panel on Nutrition of the Elderly. HMSO London.

Anthropometrics

Anthropometric measurements are a useful means of assessing nutritional status when interpreted correctly. They have the advantage of being easily obtained in the field, and large numbers of people can be surveyed in this manner. The field workers must be trained in the correct use of the equipment as incorrect measurements can give misleading results. For example, when measuring heights, workers must be aware that faulty posture can give a lower height than the actual height of the subject, and time of day is important when measuring height, since fatigue leads to decrease in muscle tone, heights tend to be less when taken during the afternoon instead of the morning. Equipment must also be well maintained particularly weighing scales, which are apt to suffer when transported. Anthropometric measurements are of particular value when assessing nutritional status in children. If children do not get sufficient food they do not grow as expected. Heights and weights of children are a useful index of nutritional status but must be correctly interpreted. Obviously other environmental factors are involved and these must always be borne in mind. Data can be interpreted with the aid of charts such as the Tanner[3] charts which show normal growth curves. If height is plotted against weight, a deficit in height for age shows the child to be stunted, whereas a deficit in weight for height shows wasting. Stunting of nutritional origin is likely to be due to a long term deficiency, whereas wasting may be short term.

Skin fold thickness is another measurement which can be easily obtained provided the skin fold calipers are used correctly; the amount of subcutaneous fat gives an estimation of adipose tissue stores. Mid-arm circumference can be very easily measured, and since it changes little between 12 to 60 months, authorities such as Jelliffe[4] have used it as a measurement of thinness.

Although many people have tried to construct formulae based on anthropometric measurements which would provide an index of nutritional status, no real success has been achieved; this is probably because size and shape can be determined by genetic make up and environmental factors, as well as nutritional ones.

Morbidity and mortality figures can both be used to draw inference about nutrition in a population.

The morbidity rate is the amount of non-fatal illness recorded in a population and is obviously useful for assessing health risk, and inferences can be drawn about nutritional status. Morbidity rates are, however, subject to question, as they are not always complete, and diagnosis may be open to question.

Mortality figures give a much more reliable source of statistics from

[3]Tanner J.M., Whitehouse R.H. (1959) *Lancet* 2, 1086-8.
[4]Jelliffe D.B. (1968) *The Assessment of the Nutritional Status of the Community* WHO Geneva.

which to draw inferences about nutrition in a population. The mortality rate most often used is the infant mortality rate, ie the number of babies dying in the first year of life per 1000 live births. In most developed countries the rate is between 10 and 20 and is mainly determined by the standard of paediatric services. However, in the under developed countries the rates range from 75 to 100 and this is mainly due to malnutrition.

Baird's[5] work has shown that pre-natal mortality rates, ie the deaths of infants under one month of age, and still births, can be an indication of maternal nutritional status. Baird[6] showed that although other factors are involved, the fall in the pre-natal death rate during the 1939-45 war was due to the supplementary rations given to pregnant women.

Interpretation of data

Tables of *Recommended daily amounts of food energy and nutrients* are often used in assessing the standards of diets, but they are not designed for assessing survey results. Recommended intakes are not uniformly related to minimum need. For example a 50 per cent deficiency in protein is more severe than 50 per cent deficiency in vitamin C.

The most useful thing a dietary survey can accomplish is to point to the critical nutritional areas in which large gains of health and efficiency can be made. The Interdepartmental Committee on Nutrition for National Defence, now the Nutritional Section of the office of Internal Research, National Institute of Health, has prepared a set of guide lines, these are based on a Male 25 years old weighing 65 kg and measuring 170 cm. See *Table 2.1.*

High is a large margin of safety to prevent clinical and biochemical symptoms of deficiency. Deficient is an intake expected to be associated with definite, although not necessarily severe, physical impairment due to a deficiency of a particular nutrient in a measurable number of people.

Summary

There are various methods of assessing nutritional status, all have their limitations. Some methods are complementary to one another and can be used together successfully, eg biochemical and dietary surveys.

Running indices, and mortality rates give an indication that malnutrition exists and where, but do not give any additional information that would be helpful in implementing a programme for improving nutrition. Many other sources of information can be utilised

[5]Baird J.D. (1974) *Companion to Medical Studies* ed. – Passmore R., Robson J.S., vol iii chap. 44, Blackwell Scientific Oxford.
[6]Baird J.D. (1960) *Lancet* 2, 557.

to yield details concerning food distribution and consumption patterns. These were summarised by an WHO Expert Committee and are shown in *Table 2.2* overleaf.

Table 2.1   Guide lines for assessing nutritional status

Nutrient		Deficient	Low	Acceptable	High
Nicotinic acid	mg/day	<5	5–9	10–14	>15
Riboflavin	mg/day	<0.7	0.7–1.1	1.2–1.4	>1.5
Thiamin	mg/day	<0.2	0.2–0.29	0.3–0.4	>0.5
Ascorbic acid	mg/day	<10	10–29	30–49	>50
Vitamin A	iu/day	<2000	2000–3499	3500–4999	>5000
Calcium	mg/day	<300	300–399	400–799	>800
Iron	mg/day	<6.0	6–8	9–11	>12
Protein	g/Kg body wt	<0.5	0.5–0.9	1.0–1.4	>1.5

ICNND (1963) *Manual of Nutrition Surveys* US Govt Printing Office, Washington DC.

Table 2.2 Information needed for assessment of nutritional status

Sources of information	Nature of information obtained	Nutritional implications
1. Agricultural data Food balance sheets	Gross estimates of agricultural production Agricultural methods Soil fertility Predominance of cash crops Overproduction of staples Food imports and exports	Approximate availability of food supplies to a population
2. Socio-economic data Information on marketing, distribution and storage	Purchasing power Distribution and storage of foodstuffs	Unequal distribution of available foods between the socio-economic groups in the community and within the family
3. Food consumption patterns Cultural-anthropological data	Lack of knowledge, erroneous beliefs, and prejudices, indifference	
4. Dietary surveys	Food consumption	Low, excessive, or unbalanced nutrient intake
5. Special studies on foods	Biological value of diets Presence of interfering factors (eg goitrogens) Effects of food processing	Special problems related to nutrient utilization

6. Vital and health statistics	Morbidity and mortality data	Extent of risk to community
		Identification of high-risk groups
7. Anthropometric studies	Physical development	Effect of nutrition on physical development
8. Clinical nutritional surveys	Physical signs	Deviation from health due to malnutrition
9. Biochemical studies	Levels of nutrients, metabolites, and other components of body tissues and fluids	Nutrient supplies in the body
		Impairment of biochemical function
10. Additional medical information	Prevalent disease patterns, including infections and infestations	Interrelationships of state of nutrition and disease

WHO Report of Expert Committee on Medical Assessment of Nutritional Status Tech. Rpt. Series No. 258 (1963a)

3: Nutritional status of groups in the population

Nutritional problems which arise in modern-day Britain may be generalised – such as obesity – or may be confined to a particular section of the population. Dietary imbalances leading to these disorders may be a consequence of ignorance, poverty and/or environmental circumstances, or they may result from a conscious decision to adopt eating patterns which, although incommensurate with long-term health, are suited to current life-styles, and which offer short-term gratification. Aspects of the nutritional stakes of different sections of the population are briefly considered below.

Infants

There is a general consensus of opinion that breast feeding is the most desirable method of feeding a baby, and that the efforts of professional staff should be devoted to encouraging the establishment of breast feeding, and its continuation for up to four to six months. The advantages of breast over bottle milk are well known, but it is worth commenting on the nutritional implications.

Cows' milk is associated with a greater occurrence of eczema, gastro-intestinal disorders associated with failure to thrive, hypernatraemia and cot death. Although Hide[1] failed to show a protective effect of breast feeding in the development of eczema in the first year, he commented that asthma and bronchitis were less common.

Winter et al[2] demonstrated a relationship between prolonged bottle-feeding and the later experience of dental caries in 4 to 5 year olds. Least dental decay was seen in children who had been breast fed the longest. The practice of sweetening milk, or dipping dummies in syrups also adversely affected subsequent dental health.

One of the main problems of using modified cows' milk in infant feeding is the danger of overfeeding. Not only are formula milks calorifically more dense, but there is a tendency for them to be overconcentrated during preparation. Using a sample of over 7,000 scoop measures of baby milk, Lyall and Skipworth[3] found that 76% were

[1]Hide D.W. (1980) *Health Visitor* 53, 43.
[2]Winter G.B. (1971) *British Medical Journal* 130, 271.
[3]Lyall R., Skipworth G.E. (1980) *Health Visitor* 53, 46.

not accurate to within ±5% of the manufacturer's recommended values. The sequelae of over-concentration are uraemia and hypernatraemia, as well as excessive energy intake, leading to the development of obesity.

Obesity is the most common nutritional disorder in present-day Britain, and gives rise to more ill-health than all the vitamin and mineral deficiencies put together. Eid[4] demonstrated that the most important factor in determining obesity in childhood was the rate of weight gain in the first year, and suggested that overweight babies are more likely to become overweight children at the age of 5 to 7 years. Whilst it is accepted that there is a strong link between childhood and adult obesity, it is now obvious that there is not such a clear cut relationship between infantile and childhood obesity[5]. Many fat babies lose their excess fat in early childhood, but the age of 4 to 5 years may be critical, and, if obesity persists beyond this point, it may be difficult to lose the excess fat. Early onset of obesity is often characterised by an increase in the total number of fat cells, which once formed, cannot be reduced in number[6,7]. Recent evidence, however, suggest that the acquisition of the ultimate number of fat cells is not limited to the first years of life. Rather, the number of fat cells increases throughout the growing period, especially at times when fat is gained physiologically, such as the pre-pubertal growth spurt and the latter half of pregnancy.

As well as pre-disposing to ill-health in later life, obesity poses additional, more immediate problems. For example, obese babies are more prone to lower respiratory disorders[8].

Fat babies also present problems of diagnosis, it is not always apparent when an obese infant is suffering from dehydration, therefore treatment may be delayed, and so the obese baby is at risk.

Deficiencies, although rarer, do occur in infants. They may be physiologically related, or be associated with the deprivation of poor socio-economic conditions. In the years of depression before the Second World War, iron deficiency was very common. Mackay[9] discovered a high incidence of iron-deficiency amongst infants in London, and associated this with increased morbidity. Davidson et al[10] found that 41 per cent of the infants in their Aberdeen survey, were anaemic. Although subsequent improvement in living standards, medical care and welfare services, reduced the size of the problem, iron-deficiency still occurs.

Premature babies do not have the complete iron stores of the full-term

[4]Eid E.E. (1970) *British Medical Journal* 2, 74-76.
[5]Myres A.W., Yeung D.L. (1979) *Canadian Journal of Public Health* 70, 113.
[6]Brook C.G. (1972) *Lancet* 2, 624.
[7]Widdowson E.M., Shaw L. (1973) *Lancet* 2, 905.
[8]Hutchinson-Smith B. (1970) *Medical Officer* 123, 257-262.
[9]Mackay H.M.M. (1931) *Medical Research Council Special Report Series No. 157*
 HMSO London.
[10]Davidson L.S.P. et al (1933) *British Medical Journal* 1, 685.

baby, and thus may be more susceptible to the development of anaemia, especially if supplementary iron is not given. Megaloblastic anaemia is not uncommon amongst premature infants. This results from reduced stores – reflected in lower serum folate levels – and the increased demands due to rapid growth. Bottle-fed babies tend to have relatively lower serum folate levels, than breast-fed babies, for although humans' and cows' milk contain similar concentrations of folate, heating destroys much of this.

Deficiency of vitamin C, resulting in clinical symptoms of scurvy, is uncommon. A report by the British Paediatric Association in 1964 cited 84 cases of infantile scurvy over a two year period[11]. It suggested that handicapped children were most at risk, together with those from 'problem families'. Breast milk provides between 15 to 45 mg vitamin C daily – sufficient to prevent any signs of deficiency.

According to the Panel on Child Nutrition[12] '. . . the impression emerges that *nearly* all babies receive variable, but substantial amounts of vitamin D during the first 6-12 months of life.'

Much of this vitamin D is derived from fortified milks and cereals, the consumption of which declines rapidly after the first year of life. Rickets, when it occurs, is usually seen in slightly older children and it is discussed more fully in the next section.

Pre-school and school children

After the Second World War, the Chief Medical Officers' Committee on Medical Aspects of Food Policy recommended the instigation of nutritional surveys on various sections of the population.

A pilot survey of the *Nutrition of Young Children*[13] (1963) collected data concerning the intake of specific foods and nutrients, and also investigated the inter-relationships of nutritional, socio-economic and anthropometric factors.

A few cases of unsatisfactory physique were found, thinness and plumpness were reported on, but did not seem to relate to calorie intake. The intakes of fat, sugar and energy were greater where there were four or more children in the family, and the mean daily intake of vitamin C decreased with increasing family size. A large range of milk intakes was seen – averaging less than one pint a day, despite welfare allowances. As milk is seen to be an important source of protein, calcium and riboflavin, this low intake could be a cause for concern. The low milk intakes were reflected by low nutrient intakes – some not reaching *Recommended daily amount*. Though numbers were too small to be convincing, the survey found an apparent relationship between height and milk consumption.

[11]British Paediatric Association (1964) *British Medical Journal* 1, 1659.
[12]DHSS (1970) *Interim Report by the Panel on Child Nutrition.*
[13]DHSS (1963) *Report on Public Health and Medical Subjects No. 118*, HMSO London.

A sub-committee on nutritional surveillance was set up to advise on the detection of changes in the nutritional state of the community which could arise from the changes in 1971 of arrangements for the provision of welfare milk, school meals and school milk, and also to consider the long-term arrangements for assessing the nutritional effect of changes in government policy. The report stated that milk is an important part of the diet for pre-school children and any nutritional changes which did occur due to changes in legislation, though small, could be cumulative[14].

A further study carried out in 1967-8[15] re-affirmed the importance of milk as a source of nutrients for the younger child. In this study of children aged six months to four and a half years, average nutrient intakes exceeded *Recommended daily amounts* for all nutrients except vitamin D and iron. Seventy-five per cent of vitamin D intake was supplied by fortified milks, baby foods and vitamin supplements.

The possible relationship between milk and height, noted in the 1963 pilot survey, was not confirmed. Although there was a tendency for height to increase with milk intake, it was only slight, and not consistent. Those children drinking little milk were neither shorter nor lighter than the mean.

More recently, data from the National Study of Health and Growth has been used to further assess the relationship between height and milk[16]. It was concluded that free school milk has little, if any, effect on growth rates, and indicated that most children drank substantial quantities of milk at home.

The nutritional intake of the child depends very much on what is provided by the mother. Although this influence decreases in importance as the child gets older, it is obvious that the mother's knowledge of nutrition is instrumental in the avoidance of nutritional problems.

The annual reports of school medical officers show that during this century, there has been an increase in the growth rates of school children in the United Kingdom. Improved nutrition is undoubtedly largely responsible for this, although other factors are operating as well.

There was a significant fall in animal protein intake between higher and lower social groups, but the differences were small. A similar pattern was seen for riboflavin, though there was no significant social-class differences in intake of calcium, iron, other B vitamins, and vitamins C and D. The authors point out that many other related factors may influence food intake – such as family size and education of parents. A social class effect is well illustrated by the following example.

Between the years 1937-57, the heights of 13 to 14 year old public school boys changed little whereas those of LCC school boys of the same

[14]DHSS (1973) *Report on Public Health and Medical subjects No. 6,* HMSO London.
[15]DHSS (1975) *Report on Health and Social Subjects No. 10,* HMSO London,
[16]Cook J. et al (1973) *British Journal of Preventive Medicine* 27, 91.

age increased steadily. By 1957, LCC school boys were still, on average, 40cm shorter than public school boys. Eppright reported that height, weight and body circumference were greater in the more affluent groups, but skinfold thicknesses were greater in the poorer groups, ie they were fatter[17].

However, Cook[16] found that social class was not in general associated with highly significant differences in average intakes.

As previously mentioned, the introduction of welfare foods and supplements were largely responsible for the improvements seen, and it is of some concern that these benefits are now being gradually withdrawn.

Nutritional problems may arise at this time, or may have developed during infancy. The major ones are outlined below:

RICKETS

Rickets is a disease of growing bones and is thus most common in young children, having a peak incidence between eighteen months and three years. It may also be seen in adolescents. It is primarily due to lack of vitamin D, necessary to ensure proper calcification of the bones.

Vitamin D may be derived from dietary sources, or it can be synthesised endogenously. There are few dietary sources and notably the vitamin is lacking in human milk. This has led some workers to suggest that vitamin D is not an essential dietary substance. Indeed it can be questioned whether it is a vitamin at all, as it is produced in one part of the body, and acts in another – the hallmark of a hormone.

It is estimated that on average, about ten per cent of the vitamin D requirement is met by the diet. The rest is manufactured by the body, commencing with the action of ultra-violet light on a substance secreted under the skin.

Surveys carried out in the early part of this century indicated that over half the child population was suffering from rickets. The disease was most common in urban areas, and in children from slum dwellings. In 1923, Dame Harriet Chick published the report of her work in Vienna[18], in which she recognised the importance of the dual factors of diet and sunlight in protecting against rickets. Subsequent measures of slum clearance, pollution control and improved diet led to a dramatic decrease in the incidence of the disease. The appearance of fortified margarine, and the introduction of National Dried Milk and welfare supplements at the beginning of World War II virtually eradicated the disease. Unfortunately the initial fortification levels chosen were too high, and cases of vitamin D toxicity began to appear. The levels were then reduced; recently National Dried Milk has been withdrawn

[17]Eppright E.S. et al (1972) *World Review of Nutrition and Dietetics* 14, 219.
[18]Chick H. (1923) *Medical Research Council Special Report Series 77* HMSO London.

(through concern over electrolyte levels rather than its vitamin D content).

Rickets is now becoming more common again. An interim report published by DHSS in 1970 concluded that rickets in the British population occurs only sporadically throughout the country, and that this was in part caused by a tendency for babies to be fed on unfortified liquid milk. Also, it was apparent that misunderstandings occurred over the use of vitamin supplements, eg some mothers believed that vitamin C would prevent rickets[19].

Within the risk groups as a whole, Asians are relatively more vulnerable to rickets. A number of factors contribute to this, the most important of which are exposure to sunlight and intake of dietary vitamin D. The diets of Asian immigrants contain even less dietary vitamin D than those of the Caucasian population, and vitamin supplements are less likely to be used. Exposure to sunlight is diminished, due to environmental and cultural factors as well as by skin pigmentation.

Cranston and Williams describe an outbreak of rickets at a girls school in Leicester, showing that this is indeed a contemporary nutritional problem[20].

ANAEMIA

There is much evidence to indicate that iron deficiency anaemia is not uncommon amongst children. Arneil in Glasgow[21] and Gans in London[22], both reported on the condition, and the DHSS pilot survey of 1963 included a special investigation of haemoglobin levels, when an incidence of ten per cent anaemia was seen. Low average intakes of iron were also seen in the DHSS 1968 survey. More recently, Black reported marginal iron as well as vitamin D intakes in pre-school children in Newcastle on Tyne[23]. Gans pointed out that iron deficiency anaemia was almost the norm amongst the West Indian population he studied.

Iron deficiency anaemia is perhaps the most widespread of deficiency diseases in Western countries. It often originates during pregnancy, when increased demands are put on the body and these extra requirements are not met by an already marginal diet. The infant fails to build up an adequate store of iron and this may be further restricted if the birth is premature. Prematurity itself may be associated with poor nutrition. Iron stores are utilised rapidly during the first few months of life as the infant's blood volume increases. Little iron is supplied by milk,

[19]DHSS (1970) *Report on Public Health and Medical Subjects No. 123* HMSO London.
[20]Cranston D., Williams G.L. (1978) *Community Medicine* 9, 3.
[21]Arneil G.C. (1969) *World Review of Nutrition and Dietetics* 10, 239.
[22]Gans B. (1967) *Proceedings of the Nutrition Society* 26, 218.
[23]Black A.E. et al (1976) *British Journal of Nutrition* 35, 105.

so that unless a good mixed weaning diet is introduced, anaemia can easily arise. In later childhood, the condition may persist as the rich dietary sources of iron are not always the most popular of foods with children, eg spinach, liver. Refined foods tend to be iron deficient, and though some, such as flour, are fortified by law, it is doubtful whether significant amounts of the added iron are absorbed.

DENTAL DECAY

Dental disease is a problem of massive proportions in this country. Todd estimates that eighty per cent of five year olds require treatment for dental caries, and about ten per cent of all children enter school with more than half of their teeth seriously decayed[24].

The caries rate in pre-school children is lower than in older children, though this probably just reflects the length of time of exposure to cariogenic foods[25].

Whilst fluoridation of water supplies seems to be the best single preventative measure that can be taken, there is also the nature of the diet to be considered. Since the early part of this century, there has been a massive rise in the consumption of refined sugar. Sweet, sticky foods will adhere to the teeth, producing an ideal environment for bacteria to initiate decay processes. It does seem though, that the number of times sugar is consumed is more important than the absolute amount.

OBESITY IN CHILDHOOD

Abraham and Nordesieck examined 200 school children, half of normal weight and half obese, with 50 boys and 50 girls in each group[26]. They re-examined the sample twenty years later and found that of the original group of obese boys, 86% were still overweight, whilst only 42% of the 'normal' group had become overweight. Comparative figures for the girls were 80% and 18%. They also found that markedly overweight children were more likely than moderately overweight children to become obese as adults. There is a strong tendency for obesity to recur after initial weight loss, and then to persist into young adult life.

To date, there have been few systematic studies on the aetiology, prevalence, treatment or prevention of obesity in children. One study, of 2,500 school children in Buckinghamshire classified 32.4% of 14 year old girls and 3.6% of 14 year old boys as obese[27].

The major environmental causes of obesity are excess food intake and reduced energy expenditure due to decreased physical activity. The older one gets, the more difficult it becomes to lose weight. It would seem

[24]Todd J.E. (1975) *Childrens Dental Health in England and Wales 1973* OPCS HMSO London.
[25]Binns N.M. (1979) *Getting the most out of Food No. 14* Van den Burghs and Jurgens.
[26]Abraham S., Nordesieck M. (1960) *Public Health Reports 75*, 263.
[27]Colley J.R.T. (1974) *British Journal of Preventive Social Medicine 28*, 221.

to be a worthwhile investment to put much effort into tackling childhood obesity, forestalling later failure in treatment and perhaps reducing the incidence of circulatory and skeletal disorders.

POOR NUTRITIONAL STATE

Vitamin deficiencies are now rare as a form of malnutrition in this country, and cases that do arise are due to neglect, ignorance or language difficulties. Cook[16] reported that there was little evidence of clinical nutritional deficiency. A more common form of malnutrition may be decribed as 'poor nutritional state' and is characterised by smallness for age, poor muscle development and muscle tone, thinness and pallor with little desire for voluntary exercise, and lacking *joie de vivre*[28].

It may be that the presence or absence of deficiency states is too crude an index of nutritional status, whilst the assessment of milder and less specific states of malnutrition is at present too subjective. In the future, biochemical tests may be used more extensively to assess nutritional status.

Adolescents

As children get older they assume more responsibility for their own food intake or influences from outside the home begin to have a more significant effect. Dietary patterns may be influenced by social and psychological factors, time available, and economic considerations. An outline of these is given by Lennon and Fieldhouse[29]. The Ten States Survey in the United States found more evidence of unsatisfactory nutritional status amongst 10 to 16 year olds, than in any other age group[30].

Obesity continues to be a problem and a suggestion of a prevalence of about 10 per cent obesity in adolescent girls, is probably a conservative estimate. The image of slimness is established as the norm for adolescent girls in our culture, and this undoubtedly contributes to the negative feelings often expressed by overweight girls. Even girls who are not overweight, commonly wish to lose weight and if this results in a restricted nutritional intake, then there is a cause for concern. The filling-out process which occurs at puberty may result in a temporary plumpness until growth and weight is stabilised, but once obesity has developed, a life-style of social isolation and physical inactivity tends to maintain the obese state. Bullen compared a group of obese adolescent girls with non-obese controls and found that the obese girls were less independent, and though aware of their inactivity, had no realistic

[28]Darke S.J. (1972) *Nutrition* 26, 1 p24-31.
[29]Lennon D., Fieldhouse P. (1979) *Community Dietetics* Forbes London.
[30]USDHEW (1972) *Publication no. (HSM 72-8134)* Govt Printing Office Washington DC.

concept of how inactive they were, or that inactivity may be related to obesity[31]. Being overweight was connected solely with excessive food intake.

Dieting behaviour may be more related to attempts to achieve the ideal 'fashion model' image, than because of primary concern with weight. Inappropriate and excessive attempts at weight-loss may precipitate problems of anorexia nervosa.

Anorexia nervosa describes a disorder of complex aetiology and effect. It is defined by weight loss of at least 25 per cent of original body weight, or at least 15 per cent less than normal weight for age and height, and involves distorted self-image.

It has an associated morbidity rate of 10 to 15 per cent, and thus should be viewed with great concern. Although the causes are manifestly psychological in origin, the consequences are seen in physical wilful refusal to eat and pre-occupations with food and weight loss are characteristic. Bruch describes how anorexia nervosa is a struggle for self-control, effectiveness and self-identity, with thinness being only an accidental by-product of these efforts[32]. Alternatively, food may be seen as a symbol of developing feminity, and rejection of food is equivalent to rejection of womanhood. By dieting, the body is maintained in a pre-pubescent state.

Selective nutritional deficiency may arise from poorly balanced diets brought about by restricted food preferences, food aversions, religious tenets or weight-reducing regimes. Some cult diets may be harmful, leading to a number of deficiency diseases. The Zen Macrobiotic diet, when based solely on cereals, is claimed to promote health and cure such ailments as cancer and heart disease. Instead, the result is scurvy, anaemia, hypoproteinaemia, and other forms of malnutrition. Because of the fluid restriction imposed, there have been cases of kidney failure and even death[33].

Anaemia due to iron deficiency continues to be widespread. During adolescence there is an increased requirement for iron, occasioned by the growth spurt, and in females extra iron is needed to compensate for the losses through menstruation. More efficient iron-absorption may help to ameliorate some of this increased demand, whilst dislike of iron-rich foods reduces dietary intake.

For similar reasons, calcium intake may need to be carefully monitored. Increased requirements to allow proper growth, and substitution of squashes and minerals for milk, show why this is so. Heald suggests that low calcium intakes during the adolescent growth

[31]Bullen B.A. et al (1963) *American Journal of Clinical Nutrition* 12, 1.
[32]Bruch H. (1974) *Eating Disorders: Obesity, Anorexia Nervosa and the Person Within* Routledge & Kegan Paul, London.
[33]Katchadourian H. (1977) *The Biology of Adolescence* W.H. Freeman, San Francisco.

phase may weaken the bone structure, and pre-dispose to osteoporosis in later life[34].

Associated with calcium restriction may be vitamin D deficiency, resulting in a secondary peak in the incidence of rickets at the time of adolescence. Increased metabolic requirements due to growth may contribute to the development of other mild vitamin deficiencies, particularly of vitamins A and C. The Ten States Survey indicated that young people, in all socio-economic and ethnic groups, exhibited a high prevalence of low vitamin A levels, though it was more strongly associated with poverty and minority ethnic groups. Vitamins A and C were also pin-pointed by the Health and Nutrition Examinations Survey of 1974[35].

The nutritional problem of adolescents seem to have received relatively little attention in Britain. Because this is a major period of physiological growth, nutritional intake is of paramount importance. Also, there may be consequences for later health, difficulties in pregnancy, coronary heart disease in middle-age and perhaps osteoporosis in old-age.

Pregnancy

Nutritional deficiencies during pregnancy may reflect inadequate intakes over the preceding years, being precipitated by increased requirements at this time of physiological stress. Iron and vitamin D intakes are commonly well below those recommended. Whilst milder shortfalls in other vitamins may well be associated with low energy intakes. Low social class and early age of pregnancy both seem to be associated with poorer nutritional intakes[36].

Extreme nutritional deprivation during pregnancy is likely to have severe effects on the developing foetus, being manifested as retarded physical and mental developments. However, many physiological and nutritional adaptations occur during pregnancy, and a wide range of dietary intakes are compatible with the normal growth and development of the baby. Weight gain may be taken as an indicator of satisfactory nourishment, though whilst 12.5 kg is normally viewed as being the desirable gain for the whole of pregnancy, gains of 0 to 40 kg have been associated with normal births.

Extra iron is needed for the foetus and placenta, and for the increased red cell mass of the mother. If dietary intake is inadequate, the foetus still has priority, and the mother can become severely anaemic. Chanarin suggests that megaloblastic anaemia in pregnancy is the most sensitive

[34]Heald F. (1969) *Adolescent Nutrition and Growth* Butterworth, London.
[35]USDHEW (1974) *Publication No. (HRA 74-1215)* Govt Printing Office, Washington DC.
[36]Smithells R.W. et al (1973) *British Journal of Nutrition* 38, 497.

index of the nutritional folate status of a population[37]. It reflects folate status before pregnancy, and exhibits socio-economic class differences, and seasonal variations – due to availability of vegetable sources of the vitamin.

The frequency of megaloblastic anaemia among Indian immigrants to Britain is about three times that in the white population[38]. Vegetarianism is the factor responsible for low serum vitamin B_{12} levels found in Hindus and though low level *per se* are not incommensurate with normal health, low plasma levels in the mother can lead to the development of severe deficiencies in the infant.

As pregnancy is a time of close medical surveillance the opportunity exists for detection and corrections of nutritional deficiencies. As nutritional status may influence the reproduction efficiency of a population, this is an area which merits more attention both from clinical nutritionists and those concerned with nutritional education.

Elderly

Nutritional requirements do not differ greatly in old-age from those of younger adults. There may be a reduced need for energy as and if energy expenditure declines. Malnutrition, when it occurs, is likely to be part of an overall picture of dehabilitation though sub-clinical deficiencies may be more widespread.

Dietary intake in the elderly is influenced by a range of physical, social and psychological factors, illustrated in *Figure 3.1.*

Figure 3.1   Factors influencing dietary intake of old people

Physical	Disability
	Rheumatism
	Inadequate dentures
Social	Loneliness
	Social isolation
	Type of housing
	Shopping facilities
	Reduced income
Psychological	Depressive illness
	Bereavement
	Food faddism

[37]Chanarin I. (1973) *Nutritional Deficiencies in Modern Society* ed-Howard A.N. Newman, London.
[38]Britt R.P. et al (1970) *Quarterly Journal of Medicine* 40, 499.

There have been several large-scale studies concerned with the nutrition of the elderly, notably, those carried out by the DHSS, and those of the King Edward Hospital Fund. The first report by the Panel on Nutrition of the Elderly concluded that the number of malnourished elderly people was probably small, and did not constitute a serious problem[39].

The nutrients most likely to be deficient in the diet of an elderly person are vitamins C, D, the B vitamins and iron. Although frank signs of scurvy are rare, low blood levels of vitamin C are not uncommon amongst the elderly. They result from low dietary intake, particularly in institutions, which suffer the problem of large-scale food preparation. Low serum levels of vitamin C have been linked with depressive illness, and this in turn may lead to a dis-inclination to obtain, prepare, or even eat food. Certainly, it does not help to mitigate the effects of iron-deficiency, resulting in anaemia.

Old people living on their own and under poor economic circumstances sometimes show evidence of folate deficiency, though the occurrence of nutritional megaloblastic anaemia is uncommon. Assessment of folate status is difficult to measure, and complex inter-actions are evident. For example, while deficiency of iron or of vitamin C, lead to lower serum folate levels, deficiency of Vitamin B_{12} has the opposite effect. Malabsorption may also reduce blood folate levels, and there is some evidence that a primary deficiency of folic acid may itself cause malabsorption syndrome, thus establishing a downward spiral of decreased intake and decreased absorption.

Subclinical deficiencies of riboflavin, thiamin and pyridoxine may occur in elderly populations[40], and could be associated with the generalised symptoms of anorexia, malaise and irritability seen in elderly people.

It may be concluded that old people with low vitamin levels may at least be in the process of developing physical changes; and attention should be given to detecting and rectifying this situation.

Vitamin D deficiency may arise through a variety of reasons, including poor dietary intake, malabsorption, and inadequate exposure to sunlight. Calcium absorption is thus impaired, leading to the development of osteoporosis and increased liability to fractures.

Osteomalacia is also seen – detected in 4 per cent of elderly women admitted to geriatric wards[41]. The relationships between vitamin D deficiency and skeletal rarefaction are not clearly delineated, but the possibility that dietary supplementation may reduce the incidence of bone disorders amongst the elderly indicates the need for further studies.

[39]DHSS (1970) *Report on Public Health and Medical Subjects No. 123* HMSO London.
[40]Vir S.C., Love A.H.G. (1977) *International Journal of Vital Nutritional Research* 47, 325.
[41]Anderson I. et al (1966) *Scottish Medical Journal* 11, 429.

4: Current nutritional theories

This chapter does not seek to discuss in great detail the current hypotheses on diet and disease, merely to put forward some of the nutritional issues that are of concern at the moment. Many of these theories have come to the attention of the media, and thus to the public's attention. Unfortunately many misconceptions have arisen, and some of these have been exploited by the food manufacturers as a means of promoting new products and increasing their markets.

Alcohol

Alcohol has been with us since prehistoric times; it was probably discovered when some forgetful cavemen left some cereal out in the rain and then forgot about it, remembering it some time later and eating it, with no doubt very surprising results. Each country has its own types of alcoholic drink, depending upon the cereals and fruits available, eg whereas Scotland has whisky made from the distilled products of fermented barley, Japan has sake, which originates from rice. Spirits are produced in most countries by distillation, but in the USA, an interesting method was evolved for the production of applejack. The wine made from apples would be left outside in the winter and the ice formed would be removed concentrating the alcohol content. Thus the harder the winter, the more potent the applejack!

ALCOHOL CONSUMPTION AND GOVERNMENT REVENUE

Alcohol consumption in Great Britain provides considerable revenue for the government from the tax which is levied on it. It is interesting to see how much revenue is derived from alcohol taxation and to note that while cigarettes carry a health warning alcohol does not. In the early 1970s the alcohol industry had an invested income of 1,700 million pounds, 4.9% of the gross national product.

Table 4.1 Spirits: Quantities retained for consumption and net receipts of duty

Net receipts £	Quantity home produced million proof gallons	Quantity imported million proof gallons
1970/71 – 371,684 million	15,356	4,709
1976/77 – 869,138 million	27,598	7,288

The revenue from tobacco 1976/77 was 17.2% of the net receipts of the customs and excise and alcohol 17.9% whereas in 1966/67 the revenue from tobacco was 28.3% of the customs and excise, and alcohol 19.0%[1].

Spirit consumption has, if we look at *Table 4.1*, risen during the years from March 31st 1970 to March 31st 1977 by 14,821 million proof gallons.

Beer consumption in 1970/71 was 34.92 million bulk barrels and in 1976/77 was 40.82 million bulk barrels (a bulk barrel is 36 gallons).

PHYSIOLOGICAL AND NUTRITIONAL EFFECTS

Ethanol (ethyl alcohol) is readily absorbed from the gastrointestinal tract and can be used by the body as an energy source providing 7 kcals/g. It differs from carbohydrate and fat in that it cannot always be utilised by the muscle and it is almost entirely metabolised by the liver at a fixed rate which is not affected by concentration of alcohol in the blood. Alcohol in the liver is oxidised under the influence of alcohol dehydrogenase to acetaldehyde, this is then oxidised to acetic acid and thence to carbon dioxide and water, or the acetic acid enters the citric acid cycle to be converted to fatty acid.

The mechanisms of liver injury has been ascribed to the toxicity of alcohol, malnutrition, genetic predisposition and hypersensitivity reactions or a combination of all these factors. Work done by Lieber and Rubin (1968) shows that the most important fact is its toxicity[2].

The effect of alcohol on physical and mental behaviour is not always understood by the general public. Many think that alcohol is a stimulant whereas in reality it is a depressant. *Table 4.2* shows the effect of alcohol on mental and physical behaviour.

ALCOHOLISM

We tend to think of alcoholism as a modern disease, but it has been evident for hundreds of years. Alcoholism as a disease presents problems of definition. Sociologists define it in terms of the adverse effects of alcoholism on the family or society; psychiatrists in terms of its effect on the personality of the alcoholic and addiction, while physicians are mainly interested in the effect on the liver and the other organs of a chronically high alcohol intake.

However, all these above methods of defining alcoholism are valid but rarely does one effect occur without another. the World Health Organisation (WHO), after much discussion, produced a definition of alcoholism, 'alcoholism is any form of drinking which in its extent goes on beyond the traditional and customary dietary use or the compliance with the social drinking customs of the community concerned

[1]*68th Report of the Commissioners of Her Majesty's Customs and Excise for the year ending 31st March 1977* HMSO London.
[2]Lieber C.S., Rubin E., (1968) *New England's Journal of Medicine* p278-869.

Table 4.2 Effect of alcohol on mental and physical behaviour

No. of drinks	Blood alcohol level after 1 hour	Effect
1 pint beer	30mg	Likelihood of having an accident starts to increase
1½ pints beer	50mg	Impairment of judgement and inhibition
2½ pints beer or 5 whiskies	80mg	Loss of driving licence
5 pints beer or 10 whiskies	150mg	Loss of self control exuberance, slurred speech, quarrelsome
6 pints beer 15 whiskies	200mg	Stagger, double vision, memory loss
¾ bottle of spirits	400mg	Oblivion, sleepiness, coma
1 bottle of spirits	500mg	Death possible

irrespective of aetiological factors leading to such behaviour and irrespective also of the extent to which such aetiological factors are dependent upon genetic constitution or acquired physiopathological and metabolic influences'. This was later defined as excessive drinking and alcoholics were redefined as these excessive drinkers whose dependence on alcohol attained such a degree that it has a noticeable mental disturbance or an interference with their bodily and mental health, their inter-personal relations and their smooth social and economic functioning or shows the predominant signs of such development. They therefore require treatment[3].

Although some 30 studies on the prevalence of alcoholism have been performed in Great Britain, the results are inaccurate or misleading, mainly because of difficulties in definition and reporting. It was not until this century that the clinical effects of alcohol abuse were drawn to the attention of the public. Concern had previously been shown about the social effects of alcohol, much of the poverty and the criminality in the eighteenth century was attributed to alcohol; this was because the urban poor were malnourished, unemployed and in poor housing and they had recourse to cheap spirits, usually gin. The National Council on Alcoholism say that during the past ten years admissions to psychiatric hospitals for alcoholism or alcoholic psychosis have nearly doubled.

Many different factors have been suggested as possible causes of alcoholism and it is probable that it has a multifactorial aetiology. This is borne out by the interesting point that the incidence of alcoholism in

[3]WHO (1952) *Technical Report Series 48* WHO.

various groups appears to alter at various times of social stress, eg recently we have been warned by authorities such as National Council on Alcoholism that more teenagers are becoming alcoholics, this coincides with a period of high youth unemployment. In 1975/76 a study carried out in Nottingham showed that 48 per cent of boys and 39 per cent of girls aged 13 to 16 had at least one alcoholic drink during the week they were interviewed. Some cultures are known to have a very low rate of alcoholism, eg the Jewish culture have a very low rate of alcoholism but they do use alcohol nevertheless. Other groups show a high rate of alcoholism, eg Irish Americans, where the men tend to drink in secret. Attitudes to alcoholism in societies vary, eg there is a very ambivalent attitude towards alcohol in the USA: in some states alcohol is banned and in others it is legal. In Scotland a man is considered to be masculine if he can take a considerable amount of alcohol, but is subject to ridicule if he loses control.

Although alcoholics obviously produce a disruptive effect on the family, they also have an effect on the community, becoming unable to work and often necessitating hospital admissions. The high accident rate due to drunk driving is well known. It is thought that road accidents involving alcohol are costing the country £100 million a year.

TREATMENT

Traditionally in England, alcohol control has been by licensing and taxation, started in 1751 with the first large tax on gin, but this does not meet the problem of alcohol abuse. Alcoholics Anonymous was first set up in this country in 1947 and it is a voluntary body which provides support for both the alcoholic and his family. In 1965 the National Council on Alcoholism was founded, its aims are primarily educational and referral. There are also established alcohol information centres, and some specialised units dealing with alcoholics on a daily basis.

Psychiatric hospitals deal with most alcoholics requiring in-patient admissions and many have specialised units. Treatments are two-fold, based first on the treatment of withdrawal symptoms and secondly on the psychotherapy and drugs to make it easier for the alcoholic to abstain. Obviously, much more research is needed into both the natural history of the disease and its treatment, so that preventative policies can be evolved.

PRESENT POLICY

Although heavy drinking, alcoholism and drunkenness have declined considerably since the early 1900s, since the Second World War there has been a steady increase in drunkenness, consumption of alcohol and the pathological effects of drinking, and cirrhosis of the liver. Health education must make the public more aware of the dangers of alcohol abuse. However, until the government can be persuaded that the problem needs a different approach to that of taxation, then health educationalists are likely to have a hard task before them.

There is much disagreement about how to prevent alcohol abuse. Sir Nicholas Bonsor, Conservative MP for Nantwich, introduced a Private Members Bill into Parliament in 1979 which sought to allow Public Houses more flexible opening hours and to provide family accommodation in certain bars. This latter proposal was also put forward by the Erroll Committee in 1972, who also suggested snacks as well as alcohol and soft drinks ought to be provided. Neither of these proposals have been acted upon. Sir Bernard Braine, spokesman for the National Council on Alcoholism, is opposed to any relaxation of legislation, and would like to see alcoholic drinks withdrawn from the 'impulse-buying' shelves of supermarkets.

Fats

Fat is a dietary component about which many of the public are confused. Many consumers believe that oils such as corn oil and olive oil are not only physically different from hard fats such as butter and lard, but also contain less energy.

Fats in food stuffs are mainly in the form of triglycerides, which are esters of glycerol and fatty acids. There are many different fatty acids and it is they that give fats in foodstuffs their own particular characteristics. There are three kinds of fatty acids: saturated fatty acids where there are no double bonds present in the carbon chain, such as in butter; monounsaturated fatty acids with only one double bond, such as in olive oil, and polyunsaturated fatty acids (PUFA) with two or more double bonds such as in corn oil. The degree of saturation of fat determines their physical nature, ie whether they are liquid or solid at room temperatures. Fats with mainly saturated fatty acids present are solid at room temperature, while those with predominantly unsaturated acids are liquid at room temperature. This property is used in the production of margarine from vegetable oils. The fats are hardened by the action of hydrogen in the presence of a catalyst, this hydrogenation converts most of the unsaturated fatty acids into saturated fatty acids.

DIGESTION AND ABSORPTION

Fat is digested in the small intestine, but prior to that it has the effect of delaying stomach emptying, thus a fatty meal gives a feeling of satiety for a longer period of time than does a meal containing negligible fat.

Fats are first emulsified in the duodenum in the presence of bile salts, small quantities of fatty acids and pancreatic lipase. The pancreatic lipase then splits the triglycerides present into diglycerides, monoglycerides and glycerol.

The fatty acids and monoglycerides pass into the cells of the mucous membrane as micelles. Further hydrolysis may take place in the cells and the long chain fatty acids are re-esterified into new triglycerides, these new triglycerides are typical of human triglycerides (apparently if one animal – the pig – is fed large amounts of one particular fat source eg fish oil, it does not always convert it to its own triglycerides).

The new triglycerides enter the lacteals of the small intestine where they are in the form of chylomicrons, from there they pass into the mesenteric lymph vessels, enter the thoracic duct and join the systemic circulation via the right subclavian vein.

Cholesterol, although present in most Western diets (about 500mg/day), is synthesised in the body, mainly in the liver. Cholesterol is excreted unchanged in the bile and is oxidised in the liver to bile acids, these are the sources of loss of cholesterol. Cholesterol metabolism is subject to feed back control, in that when dietary cholesterol increases, endogenous synthesis is suppressed and breakdown of cholesterol is increased. Cholesterol levels in the plasma usually fall when a diet low in cholesterol is taken but this does not always persist.

REQUIREMENTS FOR FAT

Apart from its satiety value fat has other functions in the diet, the majority of people in the world use fat to make food more palatable and vary their menus. Fat has a high energy content 9 kcals/g, thus it is particularly useful in people requiring a high energy intake. Fat also provides a vehicle for the fat soluble vitamins. The food industries use fat as an anti-staling agent in bread, it also makes a softer product.

Although in most countries fat contributes 15 to 45 per cent of the total energy (the lower figure represents the poorer countries) it is not really known what recommendations should be made for the amount of fat necessary for health. Probably at least 20 per cent of energy should come from fat; this would provide the necessary fatty acids and give some satiety but this minimal figure is certainly not well tolerated in the UK. During World War II the fat intake was reduced to 33 per cent of the total energy, this gave rise to much more discontent than any other rationing.

Current US guidelines recommend that fat consumption should be reduced to provide only 30 per cent of total energy intake[4].

FAT INTAKES

Primitive man in his mesolithic stage was a hunter and his diet could probably be compared with that of the Eskimo and Masai. The diet was high in fat of animal origin and low in carbohydrates.

In the Middle Ages in the United Kingdom the wealthy had a higher fat intake than did the poor. Even though most households had a cow and a pig, the pig would be slaughtered to last through the winter months.

[4]*US Senate Select Committee on Nutrition and Human Needs* (1977) Govt Printing Office Washington DC.

After the Industrial Revolution the urban poor had a very inadequate diet, low in fat as well as other nutrients. Although Lloyd 'points out that milk consumption per head was no lower in 1835 than in 1935, the distribution was mainly concentrated in rural areas due to transport difficulties'[5].

Rationing of fats was carried out in both World Wars, in the First World War, butter and margarine were limited to 4 to 5 oz per head per week. During World War II rationing of fats gradually reduced the energy derived from fats to 33 per cent of total energy by 1947. When rationing ceased in 1954 the energy derived from fats rose from 38.9 per cent in 1954 to 41.7 per cent in 1976[6].

FAT AND ISCHAEMIC HEART DISEASE (IHD)

It was Keys in 1953[7] who first suggested that fat intakes in various countries correlated with the incidence of IHD in those countries. In 1970 Keys published the findings of his *Seven Countries Study*[8] and found a strong correlation with intake of saturated fats and IHD. There were very positive correlations between dietary saturated fat and plasma cholesterol and between plasma cholesterol and IHD.

Easty[9] showed a correlation between habitual total intake of fat, percentage of total energy derived from fat and plasma cholesterol, but his studies were conducted over the period of one year and repeated measurements were taken. Other workers have also found it necessary to take repeated measurements to demonstrate this. However, in 1977 in a postscript to the study carried out over the period 1956/66 showed that middle-aged men in the survey who had a high energy intake had a lower rate of IHD, and men who had a high intake of dietary fibre had a lower rate of IHD. Although fewer cases of IHD developed in men with a relatively high ratio of PUFA to saturated fatty acids in their diet, the difference was not statistically significant.

In 1974, the DHSS published a report on *Diet and Coronary Heart Disease*[10] and concluded in the section dealing with fat that the high consumption of fat was likely to be an important factor in the incidence of IHD among the relatively inactive and well nourished population in the UK. The issue is complicated by the fact that people who consume a high fat diet are often cigarette smokers and tend to have high sucrose intake. The evidence was not clear cut on the advantages of using polyunsaturated fatty acids. The Panel made various dietary recommendations, namely that obesity should be avoided (fats are

[5]Lloyd (1936) *Journal of Proceedings of Agricultural Economics Society* vol iv, No. 2.
[6]MAFF *Household Food Consumption and Expenditure Annual Report of the National Food Survey Committee* HMSO London.
[7]Keys A. (1953) *Journal of Mount Sinai Hospital* 20, 118.
[8]Keys A. (1970) *Seven Countries Study* Circulation 41 Supplement 1.
[9]Easty D.L. (1970) *British Journal of Nutrition* 24, 307.
[10]DHSS (1974) *Diet and Coronary Heart Disease* No. 7 HMSO London.

implicated in the aetiology of obesity – see later); and that saturated fat in the diet should be reduced. No recommendation was made about increasing PUFA. The panel also recommended sucrose consumption should be decreased.

FAT AND OBESITY

As mentioned previously one of fat's important functions as far as the consumer is concerned is that it can help make food more appealing and improve flavour. However, since fat is such a concentrated source of energy it can contribute very easily to an excess energy intake.

Many people since they do not see the fat present in food are not always aware how much fat there is. For example, cracker type biscuits contain a high proportion of fat but it is not evident.

Cutting down on fat intake and hidden sources is a valuable method of reducing weight in the obese and decreasing the likelihood of IHD.

Fibre

Man has produced cereals since prehistoric times, when neolithic man learned to grow crops. Cereals were at first merely ground between stones to produce a coarse meal and this was so for a long period of time. It is thought that sieving to remove the very coarse chaff was first carried out in Egypt. The Greeks and Romans used sieves of linen and wool but these were still primitive and the meal produced very coarse. It was not until the eighteenth century that fine silk threads were used in sieves which removed more of the bran, leaving a product similar to our wholemeal flour. By 1878 new steel roller mills had been introduced into Britain from the Continent and the new fine silk sieves were in use, so that a much more refined flour was produced. The whiter flour was usually consumed in most cultures by the upper classes. Rye, oats and maize have never been used to produce such a low extraction flour as has wheat.

Wheat is first processed by removing the chaff, the wheat is then cleaned and milled. Wholemeal flour is produced by grinding the wholewheat kernel and is 100 per cent extraction and thus contains more crude fibre (2.0%) than the 70 per cent extraction white flour which contains only 0.1% crude fibre.

Oats are more highly milled producing oatmeal 1.1% crude fibre or rolled oats 0.9%. Rice can be processed by two main methods. The first entails parboiling the rice before removing the husk, by this method most of the vitamins and a moderate amount of crude fibre, 0.7%, are retained. The modern method of processing involves milling which removes most of the bran and then polishing in a brush machine which reduces the crude fibre to 0.2%.

WHAT IS DIETARY FIBRE?

Trowell[11] defined dietary fibre as the remnants of the plant cell wall that are not hydrolysed by the alimentary enzymes of man. Dietary fibre should not be confused with crude fibre which is mainly cellulose and a small amount of hemicellulose and lignin. The term dietary fibre is used currently, but other terms used to describe it have been unavailable carbohydrate and roughage. Dietary fibre is composed of pectins, hemicellulose and lignin. Cellulose is the substance responsible for support in plants. It is a polymer of glucose units but cannot be digested by humans although some fermentation occurs in the large bowel due to bacterial action. The hemicelluloses are a group of polysaccharides which include pentosans, xylans and galactans. They are not available to humans but are slightly more broken down by bacteria in the colon. Lignin is totally indigestible and is found in woody plant tissues. Pectins are found in fruits and are responsible for setting in jams. It must be noted that not all dietary fibre has the same composition and some sources of fibre contain other components, such as phytates which have an effect on nutrition.

CHANGES IN FIBRE INTAKE IN UK

In 1770, wheat flour consumption was approximately 500g/day. It was stoneground wholemeal flour and this level of intake meant a cereal crude fibre intake of 2.5 to 10g a day[12]. By 1870 wheat flour consumption had fallen to approximately 375g/day and its crude fibre content to 0.2 to 0.5 per 100g[13], so that crude fibre intake was 1.3g/day.

By 1970 wheat flour consumption had fallen to 200g a day and the crude fibre intake to 0.1g/100g[14], a fall in the crude fibre intake to 0.2g/day. Obviously this last figure applies to those people who ate only white flour and white bread, but in 1970 this was the majority of the population.

Previously other cereals had contributed fibre to the diet such as oatmeal in porridge, but since World War II many people in the United Kingdom adopted the American type of ready prepared breakfast cereals, made usually from refined cereals.

FUNCTIONS OF FIBRE

So far we have discussed the decline in consumption of dietary fibre and what it is, but what does it do?

First of all, foods rich in dietary fibre have an effect on satiety, they take longer to eat. Compare eating a slice of wholemeal bread, with the time taken to eat a slice of white bread. Fibrous foods feel bulkier in the

[11]Trowell H. (1972) *American Journal of Clinical Nutrition* 25, 926.
[12]Hollingsworth D.F., Greaves J.P. (1967) *American Journal of Clinical Nutrition* 20, 65.
[13]Robertson J. (1972) *Nature* 238, 290.
[14]Kent N.L. (1975) *Technology of Cereals* Pergammon Press Oxford.

stomach giving a feeling of fullness. Thus it is likely that people who consume foods rich in fibre may eat less calories than their neighbours as they are satisfied with less. Southgate and Durnin[15], showed that the small bowel performs less efficiently as the fibre content increases, thus the calorific value of stools is higher on high fibre diets. Fibre also accelerates the rate of passage of small bowel contents. If we consider these facts, fibre must be seen to play a part in the aetiology of obesity.

The laxative effects of fibre have long been acknowledged, our grandparents were aware of the value of roughage as they called it. Dietary fibre helps to form a soft bulky stool which stimulates peristalsis in the bowel.

Luyken[16], shows that cereal fibre can reduce high serum cholesterol levels, if a high intake of fibre is given. However, high serum cholesterol is not necessarily an indication of risk of ischaemic heart disease.

The importance of dietary fibre in the aetiology of many Western diseases was first recognised by Surgeon Captain T.L. Cleave, who encouraged Denis Burkitt to undertake some of the earliest research and field work done on dietary fibre. One of the first diseases where fibre was found to play an important part was diverticular disease of the colon. This disease came to the attention of the medical profession when the rising incidence of diverticulitis became apparent.

The incidence of diverticulosis (the presence of diverticuli in the bowel) has increased in the United Kingdom over the last twenty years. It is now said that 30 per cent of those over the age of 40 have the disease, over 50 per cent of those over 60 years old and 60 per cent of those over 80 years of age. It is now the commonest disease of the colon, whereas at the beginning of the century it was unknown. The changes coincide with the changes in the UK diet over the past 60 years, ie decrease in fibre content. Painter, 1964, suggested that the colon in subjects used to a high fibre intake is of wider diameter and does not develop diverticuli[17].

Burkitt[18] showed that faeces in subjects on high fibre diets were less viscous and much easier propelled along the colon, thus less pressure is engendered and diverticuli are not produced. Many gastroenterologists believe that the inclusion of more fibre in the diet would prevent or relieve the symptoms of diverticular diseases of the colon.

Fibre is now thought by many authorities, notably Burkitt, to play a part in the aetiology of diseases such as diabetes, gall stones, dental caries, cancer of the rectum and colon and others. Burkitt bases his hypothesis on the geographical distribution of these diseases and the association between lack of cereal fibre in the diet of the United Kingdom, and increase in the incidence of these diseases.

[15]Southgate D.A.T., Durnin J.V.G.A. (1970) *British Journal of Nutrition* 24, 217.
[16]Luyken R. et al (1962) *Voeching* 23, 447.
[17]Painter N.S. (1964) *Annals of Royal College of Surgeons* 34, 98.
[18]Burkitt D.P. et al (1972) *Lancet* 2, 1408.

However, as Professor Ian McDonald[19] points out the effects of fibre are not all beneficial. It is foolish to encourage speculation in the media, and by the public when much research needs to be done on its actual effect on the gut. Some authorities have suggested that a high consumption of vegetable fibre may lead to an intussusception. While a recent report claims that fibre in particular wheat bran, contains both trypsin and chymotrysin inhibitors[20].

It seems then that fibre has definite benefits in the treatment of diverticular disease of the colon, but nutritionists ought to be wary of regarding it as a panacea.

Sugar

It is interesting that one food commodity which has aroused a great deal of controversy about its effect on man, is one which is a comparatively recent addition to his diet, and that is sugar. When using the term sugar in this chapter we are referring to sucrose, or cane sugar.

The diet of prehistoric man was rich in protein, moderate in fat and poor in carbohydrate; these men were the hunters and meat eaters. The development of agriculture provided man with a readily available food source, in the form of cereals, the carbohydrate being in the form of starch mainly. Not until the seventeenth century did sugar appear in England and it was considered a luxury, chests containing sugar were usually padlocked. The establishment of sugar plantations in the West Indies and the development of the slave trade reduced the price of sugar from 1s 6d a pound to 6d a pound and it became more widely used in the homes of the rich for fruit tarts and puddings. In 1850 the world sugar production was 1½ million tons, in 1890 five million tons and now the figure is 92 million tons. Currently the consumption of sugar in the EEC is 40kg per head per year, in the USA 44kg per head per year, and the world's average is 21.1kg per head per year. Costa Rica has the highest consumption at 62kg per head per year[21].

The white sugar we use nowadays is highly refined, containing only traces of vitamins and minerals and even the brown sugars have very little nutrients in them (*see Table 4.3*).

SUGAR CONSUMPTION

Sugar consumption in the United Kingdom during the last 100 years has risen with the exception of the years during the two world wars when sugar was rationed either by the Government or by the lack of supply. Even after the war years sugar consumption rose again, showing that

[19]McDonald I. (1976) *Fibre in Human Nutrition* ed-Spiller J.A., Amen R.J. p263-269 Plenum.
[20]Mistoanaga T. (1974) *Journal of Nutritional Science Vitaminol* 20, 153.
[21]*Sugar Year Book* International Sugar Organisation.

Table 4.3 Nutritional comparison of brown and white sugars

	Energy	Protein	Fat	Retinol	Vit. D	Thiamine	Nicotinic Acid
	kcals			μg	μg	mg	mg
Sugar white per 100 g	394	Tr	0	0	0	0	0
Demerara per 100 g	394	0.05	0	0	0	Tr	Tr

McCance, R.A. and Widdowson, E.M. (1978) *The Composition of Foods* (Fourth revised and extended edition by Paul, A.A. and Southgate, D.A.T.) HMSO, London.

man finds it difficult to refrain from taking sugar. Most of the sugar currently consumed is in manufactured food products and therefore it is difficult to obtain an accurate figure for sugar consumed by an individual.

If we looked at figures for sugar consumption in the forms of table sugar and preserves in the late 1960s and early 1970s we see that sugar consumption in this form is falling.

In 1971	..	18.42 ounces
In 1972	..	17.51 ounces
In 1974	..	15.45 ounces

However, if we look at the amount of sugar consumed as preserves and sugar in 1976 and compare intakes of families with low incomes with those of families on high incomes we see that the families with the least money consume the most sugar and preserves. This is unfortunate as it means that empty calories (ie food which provides energy and little else, see *Table 4.3*) are being bought in place of other foods in homes where the diet may be marginally inadequate.

Table 4.4 Consumption of sugar and preserves 1976

1976 Income per week	Sugar and preserves per head per week
£120 +	11.07 oz
£91 – £120	13.27 oz
£57 – £91	13.43 oz
Less than £33	15.70 oz

Ministry of Agriculture Fisheries and Food 1976. *Household Food Consumption and Expenditure*. National Food Survey.

We now have the reverse situation to that in the seventeenth century when sugar was a luxury afforded only by the rich; now it is bought mainly by the poor.

SUGAR AND THE FOOD MANUFACTURERS

Sugar is, of course, an excellent preservative used as such mainly in tinned or bottled fruits and jams where it inhibits the growth of moulds and bacteria. As a preservative it is useful to the food industry as its flavour is acceptable, it is cheap and non-toxic. Sugar is also used by the food industry as a bulking agent keeping costs down. It has various properties, such as its solubility in water and its ability to caramelise, that makes it extremely useful in a whole range of food products. Sweet items are not the only foods that contain sugar – it is also used in some canned soups, pickles and sauces, presumably to enhance flavours. Manufacturers are constantly bringing out new products to tempt us into buying more manufactured foods and many, particularly sweet manufacturers, use very skilful advertising to sell their product.

Professor John Yudkin is renowned for his work on sugar and disease and the following is a brief outline of his point of view.

CORONARY DISEASE

Professor Yudkin says in his book, *Pure White and Deadly*[22] that while ischaemic heart disease obviously has a multifactorial aetiology, in his opinion sugar is an important factor. In the United Kingdom the rise in deaths from coronary disease closely follows the rise in the consumption of sugar. In South Africa the black population had little or no coronary disease, but are now beginning to show an increased incidence of the disease since the inclusion of sugar in their diet.

DIABETES

Yudkin related the number of people dying of diabetes in different countries to the amount of sugar and fat eaten some twenty years ago and found a high correlation with sugar, but not with fat[23]. He was by no means the first person to sugest a relationship between diabetes and sugar. Stocks[24] was the first in Britain to draw attention to the marked decline in diabetic mortality in two world wars which he linked with a decreased consumption of sugar.

DENTAL CARIES

Dental caries cost Britain a considerable amount in money and absences from work due to dental treatment. Together with peridontal disease it is the most common disease affecting people in the West.

Evidence suggests that in the process of tooth decay first there is a build-up of plaque on the teeth, this is made up of protein, carbohydrate food particles, deposits from saliva and bacteria. The bacteria in the

[22]Yudkin J. (1972) *Pure White and Deadly* Davis-Poynter.
[23]Yudkin J. (1957) *Lancet* 2, 155.
[24]Stocks P. (1944) *Journal of Hygiene* 43, 242.

plaque produce acid and this acid attacks the dentine until the pulp is exposed.

When readily fermentable carbohydrate is eaten the pH within the plaque can fall to 4.5 to 5.0 within 1 to 3 minutes, and it takes 10 to 30 minutes for this to approach neutrality, this produces a graph called a 'Stephan curve'[25].

These levels of acidity produce a marked increase in the solubility of the tooth enamel. It is the low molecular weight carbohydrates which produce the most rapid fall in pH; such as sucrose, glucose and fructose. Since sucrose is consumed more often than the other two, it is more cariogenic than either. The incidence of caries in children of European origin during World War II was reduced in parallel with the reduced sugar consumption. The Vipeholm study[26] was carried out on adult patients in a mental hospital who had previously had a nutritionally adequate low-carbohydrate diet. Various groups were allowed access to take sugar and toffees in different amounts and at various frequencies. The patients had, before the study, a low rate of dental caries, but it increased significantly when sucrose-containing foods were made available, particularly in those who consumed sucrose between meals.

Agencies responsible for the marketing of sugar deny there is any truth in the association of sugar with the afore-mentioned diseases. They sponsor research but not into sugar and disease, their interest has been in proving that the sugar substitutes, cyclamates, and saccharin are dangerous and ought to be banned. Indeed, the sugar bureau in America has succeeded in having cyclamates banned on very debatable evidence, whilst sugar continues to be added in unlimited quantities to all kinds of manufactured products.

Although many other factors, some of them dietary, are involved in the aetiology of diseases such as obesity, ischaemic heart disease and diabetes, sugar obviously plays a part and it is a part of our diet we could omit without upsetting the nutritional balance or causing any deficiency.

[25]Stephen R.M. (1944) *Journal of Dental Research* 23, 257-266.
[26]Gaustaffson et al (1954) The Vipeholm Dental Caries Study *Acta Odontica Scandinavia* 11, 232-364.

SECTION II

5: Patterns of consumption

There are various bodies continually monitoring food consumption and food moving into consumption in the United Kingdom. Some, such as the British Sugar Bureau, are interested because they require to have some information about consumption in order to estimate future demands. Others, like Her Majesty's Customs and Excise, produce consumption figures as a by-product of levying taxes on alcohol. However, these bodies do not give us more than a caput consumption figure at most, they do not tell us what sections of the population are actually consuming the foods and how much.

The major source of information about changing patterns of consumption in the United Kingdom is the Annual Report of the National Food Survey Committee; this report is entitled *Household Food Consumption and Expenditure* and is produced by the Ministry of Agriculture, Fisheries and Food. The figures for trends in this chapter are all derived from this source[1]. The survey is of actual household food consumption; records are kept by private households in Great Britain of food which enters the household for consumption by human members of that household.

Unfortunately the survey has to exclude soft drinks, alcoholic drinks, chocolate and sugar confectionery. These products may be bought and consumed by members of the household elsewhere, and therefore to give a figure for these items would be misleading. The survey is carried out continuously throughout the year with breaks only at Christmas, or during General Election campaigns.

Long-term trends

Consumption of foodstuffs before the Second World War was monitored by the Advisory Committee on Nutrition which produced its first report in 1937[2]. The figures produced by this body may sometimes be over-estimated as consumption of some commodities, such as milk, were based on agricultural returns. The National Food Survey was conducted during World War II but was called the Wartime Food Survey. It was at

---

[1]MAFF *Household Food Consumption and Expenditure Annual Report of the National Food Survey Committee* HMSO London.
[2]*Report of Advisory Committee on Nutrition* (1937) HMSO London.

first carried out quarterly, then on a continuous basis, from 1942. At first the survey was to include working class households only, but later households of pensioners, or those living in slum areas were included in general studies.

Table 5.1
Food consumption before and during the Second World War
per head per week

		Year	
		1935*	1944†
meat	oz.	45.0	28.4
cereals	oz.	64.6	83.3
potatoes	oz.	68.0	69.0
vegetables	oz.	35.5	39.7
fruit	oz.	35.7	9.9
milk	pints	3.3	4.0
eggs		2.9	0.9
butter/margarine	oz.	10.2	6.4
sugar	oz.	28.6	9.1

*1937 First report of Advisory Committee on Nutrition.

†1951 *The Urban Working Class Household Diet 1940-1949* First report of the National Food Survey Committee Ministry of Food. HMSO.

Before the war consumption of all foods except potatoes and cereals was increasing, in particular eggs, cheese, fruit and tea consumption was increasing, this was thought to be due to rising wage rates and falling food prices.

It is interesting that even then the Advisory Committee was recommending that some of the sugar and lightly milled cereals be replaced by potatoes.

Food control became fully operational in 1940 and the mechanics and rationale of rationing is more fully discussed in *Chapter 6*. During the war the consumption of most food items was fairly constant, but it is interesting to note the differences in consumption of some foods before and during the war. *See Table 5.1.*

As can be seen, meat consumption was almost halved; this was due to the aerial attacks on shipping making the import of meat very difficult. Cereal consumption rose, and this included bread and flour of much higher extraction rates than before the war, thus the fibre content of people's diets also rose. Potato consumption stayed the same, presumably as much was home produced anyway. Vegetable consumption rose possibly because of the 'dig for victory' campaign which urged people with gardens to use them to grow vegetables. Fruit consumption dropped to about 25 per cent of the pre-war consumption and this was due to difficulties in importing fruit. Egg consumption dropped to less than one a week, and many people saved them to make cakes; dried eggs were used by many people for the first and last time during the war.

Butter and margarine consumption were reduced but the government tried to offset the fall in butter imports by increasing production of home-produced margarine. The energy content of the wartime diet came mainly from cereals, as sugar consumption was cut by 60 per cent.

After the war

Food supplies did not become normal for some considerable time after the war, and in some cases became worse. Milk production was the first to improve and by 1949 some lifting of restrictions began, so that consumption had risen to 4.4 pints per head. Meat supplies, however, did not recover so quickly and in fact declined so that in 1949, the population in Britain was consuming 22.7 oz per head per week, a drop of 5.7 oz per head per week from the war years.

Butter supplies improved immediately after the war, and by 1949 it was possible for the government to increase the butter ration to 4 oz per person per week.

Supplies of fruit and vegetables were also quickly back to normal, although in fact tomato consumption increased by 40 per cent over pre-war intake.

Droughts in overseas countries made the supply of wheat decrease after the war and because of this the extraction rate for flour was increased to 90 per cent in 1946 for a short period. The most interesting change that occurred in consumption in the five years after the end of the war was that by 1949, although bread consumption was 61 oz per head per week compared with the pre-war level of 57 oz per head per week, flour consumption had dropped. The estimates of flour consumption before the war gave a figure of 19 oz per head per week, in 1949 the figure was 7 oz, it appeared that housewives were not baking so much. Consumption of breakfast cereals increased during these post-war years, possibly due to the influence of the American troops stationed in Britain. However, since the breakfast cereals were of a refined nature, the total effect was to reduce fibre intake.

Sugar consumption also increased during the post-war years, mainly in the form of preserves as rationing of jam ceased before that of sugar.

We have discussed at length the changes in the diet of the population in the United Kingdom before, during and after the war, because this period provides an ideal base line for comparison of long-term trends in the period 1956-1976.

Consumption trends in the period 1956 to 1976

During the ten years from 1956 to 1965, consumption of milk expanded only slightly, but compared with previous intake it had increased by 50 per cent. The abolition of cheap welfare milk and further reduction of school milk in 1971 brought about a slight increase in milk purchases. However, the real effect of these cuts was that families who were actually affected by both cuts reduced their milk intake, this was especially so in the area of welfare milk. The decrease in consumption amounted to 0.3 pints per person per week, but this is an average and the member of the household most in need might be the most deprived.

Trends in consumption of fats during the '60s and into the '70s, are complicated by the effect of shortages. In 1965 the consumption of cream had increased by 50 per cent compared with that of pre-war years, but has remained constant since.

Butter consumption has fluctuated mainly because of price fluctuations. However, during the world butter shortage in 1971 when prices were very high, butter consumption dropped from 6.0 oz in 1970 to 5.5 oz in 1971, with an increase of 0.3 oz in margarine consumption. This trend has continued, so that, in 1973 butter and margarine consumption were similar to that of 1971, and in 1976 due to phasing out of the butter subsidy, the price of butter increased by 20 per cent and consumers responded by cutting down consumption to 5.16 oz per head per week. At the same time during 1976 purchases of soft margarine rose. It is interesting that this change seems to have occurred because of economiç pressures and not because of publicity about saturated fats and health.

During the period 1956-1965, flour and other grain products were being used less, although in the following five years flour purchases increased, bread consumption continued to decrease reaching a level of 38.11 oz per head per week in 1970 compared with the figures for 1949 of 61.1 oz per head per week, and this bread in 1970 was low extraction rate white bread. This trend has continued, in that by 1973 bread purchases had declined to 33.4 oz per head per week, and by 1976 consumption was down to 33.17 oz per head per week, with a decline in the proportion of white bread bought.

Meat consumption has risen only slightly from 1965 by approximately two oz per head per week, but the proportion of poultry has also increased.

Potato consumption has declined during the '60s and '70s, thus affecting the amount of starch and fibre in the diet.

It would appear, looking at figures for household consumption, that there has been a steady decline in the amount of sugar eaten. In 1965 the figure for sugar consumption was 18.5 oz per head per week, and in 1976 it was 12.2 oz per head per week. However, this could be misleading as it is difficult to obtain figures for sugar in soft drinks, sweets and other manufactured foods eaten outside the home. Figures for sugar consumption given by the British Sugar Bureau also indicate a downward trend, but the majority of sugar and preserves are consumed by poorer families.

We have looked at long-term trends in food consumption but what does this mean in terms of nutrient intake?

Energy intake appears to be declining (*see Table 5.2*) from the 1956 figure of 2,660 kcalories per head per day to the 1976 figure of 2,280

Table 5.2 National averages for energy intake per head per day

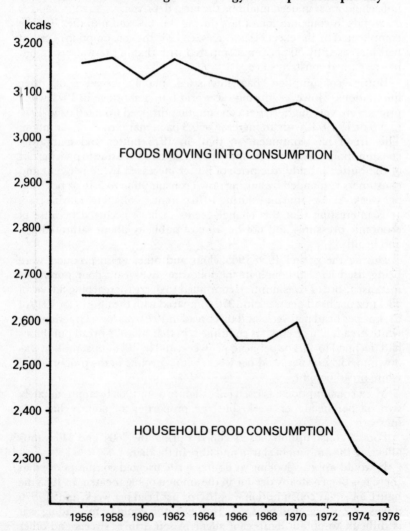

kcalories per head per day. These figures, of course, reflect only food consumed in the household; however, if we look at the energy value of foods moving into consumption, that is food available for consumption, then the trend is similar. Although a reduction of energy intake has occurred, the total fat intakes have remained remarkably constant at between 140-144 g per head per day, during the period 1956-1971, but fell to 126 g per head per day by 1976, for foods moving into consumption (*see Table 5.3*).

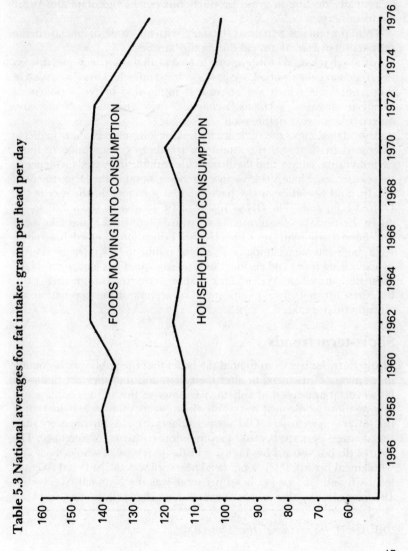

Table 5.3 National averages for fat intake: grams per head per day

Carbohydrate intake for food moving into consumption declined slowly but steadily from the figure of 422 g in 1956, to 362 g in 1976; this trend also shows in the household consumption figures where the carbohydrate value of food consumed has fallen from 364 g in 1956 to 277 g in 1976, *Table 5.4.* Since the decline in carbohydrate is greater in foods eaten in the household, it may be that the carbohydrate consumed elsewhere is mainly sugar in soft drinks, sweets, etc, as these are not included in the household consumption survey. This is further confirmed by the figures for foods moving into consumption where there is a steady decline in grain products but not in chocolate and sugar confectionery.

Total protein has remained constant, with only a slight increase in the proportion of animal protein during the late '60s.

Although it would be interesting to look at all the nutrients and discuss the trends in consumption, we have confined ourselves to a discussion of those nutrients which are at present implicated in the aetiology of Western diseases such as ischaemic heart disease, obesity and diverticular disease of the colon.

Although some of the evidence for linking long-term changes in diet is discussed in *Chapter 4* the long-term trends in consumption of fibre, carbohydrate, energy and fat do coincide with the increased incidence in these diseases. Since 1974, various agencies, notably the Department of Health and Social Security, have advised a change in the diet of the United Kingdom. The DHSS report of 1974[3] advised the public to cut down their intake of saturated fats, reduce sugar intake, and take more unrefined carbohydrates. The Health Education Council has, since 1978, been having a campaign to get the public to look after themselves by exercising more and cutting down on saturated fats and sugar. Have these had any effect? We can look at short-term trends from 1976-1979, but these do not always indicate what sectors of the population are altering their intake.

Short-term trends

Many nutritionists seem to hold the belief that the public are becoming more aware of the need to alter their diet, and that they are doing so. However, it appears that only the wealthier section of the population is buying more wholemeal and wholewheat bread, more than twice that of the lower wage earners. Old age pensioners are also buying more than the average, perhaps because they are more conscious of roughage. The figures do not show a big increase in the purchase of wholewheat and wholemeal breads. 0.65 oz per head per week was the National Average for 1976 and 0.69 oz per head per week was the National Average for 1978.

[3]DHSS (1974) *Diet and Coronary Heart Disease* HMSO London.

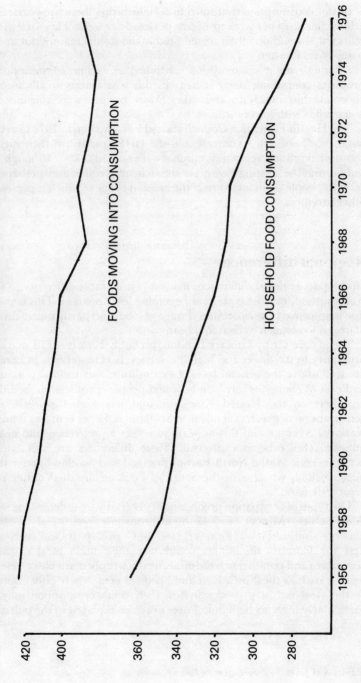

Table 5.4 National averages for carbohydrate consumption: grammes per head per day

FOODS MOVING INTO CONSUMPTION

HOUSEHOLD FOOD CONSUMPTION

49

Butter consumption continued to decline during these two years, from 5.16 oz per head per week to 4.55 oz per head per week. This pattern was reflected throughout the income groups, no doubt mainly due to the rising cost of butter.

Although sugar consumption continued to decline consumption of products containing sugar increased, this was mainly in the form of chocolate biscuits, buns and cakes. More biscuits were consumed in households with lower incomes.

The Health Education Council started its campaign in 1978 to get the nation to 'Look after Yourself' and the DHSS published their dietary recommendations regarding coronary disease in 1974. Although the public may be cutting down on sugar in tea, coffee and perhaps on cereals, people seem unaware of the amount of sugar which is present in other products.

Regional differences

In the past regional differences made a considerable difference to food consumption, but these are now becoming less apparent. This is partly due to improved transport and storage of food, and partly due to the use of frozen foods such as peas and beans.

Trends are set by Greater London, probably because of its markets, proximity to the docks and high income levels. 'Households in London are well above the general level of expenditure, quantum of purchases and cost of energy, whereas in Scotland people spent less on food than anywhere in the United Kingdom, and pay higher prices'[4]. The consumption of green vegetables in Scotland is 54 per cent less than the National Average and this appears to reflect a preference, and not an imposed choice because of costs. Taste differences are still evident between regions, the North-East of England and Scotland prefer their butter salted, whereas in the South of England unsalted butter is in greater demand.

The types of occupation predominant in certain areas determine some food habits. Miners, for example, consume one meal at least underground, and it was for this reason the Cornish pasty was evolved so that the Cornish tin miners could take their main meal of meat, vegetables and potato down the mine, neatly wrapped in a pasty case. In regions such as the North-East and Sheffield area, where either mining or the steel industry predominates, then beer consumption may be particularly high, as high fluid losses are often replaced in the pub after work.

[4]Baines A.H.J. (1979) *Proceedings of the Nutrition Society* 38, 151.

Meal patterns

Changes have occurred in the United Kingdom not only in what we eat, but when and how we eat it. W.S. Crawford Limited[5] published a survey in 1958 of meal patterns, and although certain presumptions are made in the introduction (ie the housewife knows best what to give her family) it gives an interesting comparison to present day patterns. Kelloggs sponsored a breakfast survey in 1976[6], which was carried out by Market Behaviour Limited, which gives a useful comparison to the earlier survey.

In the 1950s most adults had some form of breakfast mainly cooked (47% of the sample), but by 1976 only 19% of the adult and teenage population had a cooked breakfast. 33% had a cereal and 17% had a drink only, in the 1950s very few people (only 4% of sample) had only a drink. 40% of the population now has a cereal breakfast and 9% of children and teenagers have no breakfast at all. The omission of breakfast according to the experiments carried out in IOWA[7], where adults and children were tested physiologically, produces a poorer mental performance.

In the 1950s 60% of men, and 80% of women ate their midday meal at home, 20% of men and 8% of women ate it at work, and only 12% of men and 7% of women went to a restaurant or cafe for their evening meal. This meal would usually be cooked and of at least two courses.

The evening meal was called by a diversity of names, high tea with a cooked dish, bread, butter, jam and cakes; dinner, which was soup, main course and sweet; or tea with cakes and sandwiches.

A late supper was also taken by 75% of the population and composed of a variety of foods depending on what food was left over from the day's meals.

Little work has been done since these surveys on meal patterns. There appears to be a trend towards a cooked evening meal; afternoon tea, and high tea are not as popular as in the '50s. In the '50s people either went home for lunch or ate in the works canteen, very few went to a restaurant. Nowadays, there is another alternative, the 'take away' either as sandwiches or hot snacks. The school meal, always a subject of debate, may be replaced by a snack meal by some local authorities, changing considerably the nutritional content of the meal.

[5]W.S. Crawford Ltd. (1958) *The Foods We Eat* ed-G. Warren, Cassell, London.
[6]Kellogg Company (Great Britain) Ltd. (1976) *Breakfast and the Changing British Lifestyle*.
[7]*IOWA Breakfast Studies* (1962) US Cereal Institute.

SECTION III
Determinants of food choice

As pointed out earlier, it is true to say that personal health behaviour is the ultimate arbiter of food choice. However, this choice will be limited by a number of factors which operate at different stages during the choice process. It is possible to construct a hierarchy of determinants to illustrate this. (Figure 6.1).

The following chapters consider the various influences depicted in this hierarchy.

Figure 6.1 Hierarchy of determinants

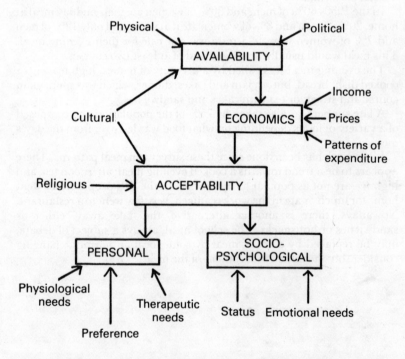

The diagram shows the main factors shaping food choice. Those nearer the bottom of the hierarchy are more a function of individual circumstances, whilst those nearer the top reflect wider societal influences and are often beyond the immediate control of the individual.

6: Availability

A fundamental limitation on food choice is simply availability, though this may be seen in terms of both cultural and physical factors. The range of foodstuffs available to a human population is governed by cultural acceptability. There are many potential sources of nutrients which are not utilised because they have never been regarded as fit for human consumption: further, foods which are thus proscribed differ between different human groups. The effect of culture on food choice is considered in detail later.

In physical terms, a comprehensive answer to the question of what is available to the British population would be whatever is produced in Britain, plus what is imported. This provides the universe of food stuffs from which individual choice can be made.

Agencies which influence food supply include government, food producers and manufacturers, and occasionally the scientific community. But first the effect of climate is briefly considered.

Climate has been one of the major determinants of which crops can be grown in different countries, and thus it has affected food choice. In the United Kingdom today because of the large amount of food that is imported, climate affects food choice less than it used to, but it can often be affected indirectly. For example, when Brazil's coffee crop was badly reduced by frost, the cost of coffee increased rapidly in the world market, and so did the cost to the United Kingdom consumer. People either paid more if they could afford it, or could not do without it, or changed to tea.

Seasonal foods such as oranges now are available all the year round, because they can be imported from different countries, although of course there will be periods of the year when oranges are cheaper because more are available.

Politics now plays a part in food availability, probably it always did but it is now more overt. Trading agreements such as with the Common Market mean that previous sources of imports such as New Zealand do not supply us with so much food, and thus foods such as lamb become more expensive. Sanctions imposed against countries may also affect availability of food; some people impose their own sanctions, refusing to buy food from a country where there is a regime of which they disapprove.

Government policies

Food policy is the complex set of decisions that government takes to influence availability, quality and price of food products to the consumer

53

(Josling 1975)[1]. According to Hirons (1980)[2] the role of the government is limited to maintaining standards – both technological and nutritional – and to preventing fraud. In order to implement controls, the Government uses advisory and educational methods – such as the publication of consumer advice, encourages voluntary codes of practice, and exerts, where necessary, full statutory controls. These include a range of taxes and subsidies designed to influence private production and consumer decisions. In extreme circumstances consumer choice can be virtually removed – as with the rationing policies of the Second World War.

A variety of legislation affects the food we eat, and indirectly our food habits. The legislation which most of the public are aware exists is *The Food and Drugs Act*, this covers food adulteration and has its beginnings in the early nineteenth century. After the Industrial Revolution food adulteration reached a peak. A chemist named Accum proved that adulteration of various food stuffs occurred and published his findings. Although a campaign was started against Accum by the brewers, legislation was eventually introduced at the instigation of the *Lancet*; this first act was entitled *The Food and Drugs Act* and was passed in 1860. The act appointed analysts but was not enforced, people were also required to pay a fee to have food analysed. In 1872, public analysts were made mandatory, so that each town had to appoint one.

The act that forms the basis of our present law was passed in 1875 and contained the provision that 'No person shall sell to the prejudice of the purchaser any article or food, anything that is not of the nature, substance or quality demanded by such purchaser'. It was this act that improved the quality of food and suppressed adulteration. *The Food and Drugs Act* has remained, with some additions such as combining public health with the act, basically the same until 1974, when the drugs aspect was superceded by the *Medicines Act* of 1968.

In the United Kingdom, it is the policy of government to reduce the use of non-nutritive substances as far as possible. 'However, it is accepted that the valuable use of additives in preserving food in that urban populations may be adequately fed, in providing technological advantages allowing the mass-production of products which could not otherwise be made on a large scale, and in producing products more acceptable to consumers because of their enhanced appearance or taste . . . requires that additives are permitted, even if controlled.' (Hirons 1980).

Food policy as we know it today did not come about until after World War II. It was at the turn of the century when Booth[3] and Rowntree[4]

[1]Josling T.E. (1975) *Nutrition* 29, 5.
[2]Hirons J.B. (1980) *Food and Health* ed- Birch G.G., Parker K.T. Applied Science Publishers.
[3]*Charles Booth's London* ed- Fried A., Elman R. (1971) Pelican Classics Penguin.
[4]Rowntree S.B. (1900) *Poverty – A Study of Town Life* Macmillan London.

published their studies on diet and poverty that attention was first drawn to the inadequacies in availability of food. This was further re-inforced when doctors examining voluntary recruits for the Boer War found 40 per cent were unfit for military service on the grounds of bad teeth, heart afflictions, poor sight or hearing, and deformities. This low recruitment rate jolted the government into taking action and the Liberal government set up an Inter-departmental Committee of Physical Health which published its report in 1904[5]. They had been asked to look into causes of ill health and they concluded that the diets of many people, especially the young, were inadequate. This resulted in the passing of the *Education Act* of 1906, which required local authorities to provide meals for needy children. The outbreak of World War I affected the civilian food supply as no previous war had done, and the food situation by 1916 was causing alarm. A Department of Food was opened at the Board of Trade with Lord Davenport at its head. At this time very little was known about nutrition and an estimate was made of minimum food requirements. The public were asked to cut down on basic foods and expected to supplement their diet with expensive ones. The general organisation of the Department of Food was poor, distribution of food was faulty and morale in the country was poor. A crisis came when German 'U' boats sank 2 million tons of shipping; Lord Davenport resigned and was replaced by Lord Rhonda, who re-organised the whole department. By 1918 civilian rationing had been introduced for the first time in Great Britain. In many cases rationing raised the feeding standards, as food was always available, at a price people could afford.

When World War II broke out the United Kingdom Government had learned from the experiences of World War I and appointed Sir Jack Drummond as the scientific adviser to the Ministry of Food. Rationing plans had been made by 1939 and ration books had been provided. Best use was made of shipping space. In January 1940, milk and fats were rationed, and gradually more foods became rationed. Certain nutritional measures were introduced, such as the fortification of margarine with vitamins A and D, and the provision of free milk, vitamins and extra eggs and meat to expectant mothers and children under 5 years. Foods off-ration included potatoes, bread, oatmeal and fish. Information was given to the housewife on how to make best use of foods available and to educate her in nutrition; this was done using posters and newspaper space. The extraction rate for flour was increased from 70 per cent to 85 per cent as wheat supplies were decreasing.

By 1944 average protein intake had risen by 6 per cent, and calcium, iron, thiamin, riboflavin, nicotinic acid and vitamin C intakes had risen considerably. There was a fall in maternal mortality rate, and infant mortality rate, as well as a general improvement in child health.

Despite the effect of the food policy carried out during the war, on the

[5]*Report of the Interdepartmental Committee of Physical Health* (1904).

health of the population the United Kingdom government has not since pursued a comprehensive policy with clear aims and objectives. Their policies which affect food, apart from *The Food and Drugs Act*, are mainly based on economic and political considerations. Indeed, at times, Ministries such as the DHSS, DES, and MAFF seem to have been pursuing opposite policies. The EEC in 1973 were subsidising butter to get rid of their butter mountain, thus decreasing the price and increasing consumption by 7 per cent. The DHSS in 1974 recommended, in its report on coronary disease[6], that saturated fats in the diet ought to be reduced. The latest EEC move is to encourage United Kingdom farmers to grow sugar beet, which will require a market, so no doubt the agencies for marketing sugar will be using advertising to make a demand for sugar, while the DHSS is trying to persuade the public to cut down sugar intake. Thompson (1978)[7] pointed out that though it may be argued that Government should do more to steer food consumption in directions believed to be beneficial to health, this is generally not politically acceptable.

Agricultural policy

Britain produces about half its own food and imports the other half. Various import regulations, trade agreements, and agricultural support schemes help to maintain the viability of this position. Home production is influenced by subsidies given to producers of certain foodstuffs in order to maintain supply even in the face of economic difficulties. These schemes could be used as a vehicle of food policy if desired.

In the United Kingdom, production of food is determined solely by economic and political considerations, unlike other countries such as Czechoslovakia, where nutrition plays an important part in determining what should be grown. The only time an attempt was made to co-ordinate agricultural and food policy was during the Second World War; the goal then was to feed the nation as well as possible.

In 1947 an *Agricultural Act* was passed, aimed at stimulation of food production by financial support and although additional schemes have been put forward since, these do not influence food choice as they have no effect on food prices paid by the consumer. As Britain is now a member of the EEC and bound by Common Agricultural Policy, there is a common tariff barrier on foods entering the EEC from non-EEC countries, this can lead to the well-known butter mountains and wine lakes. Britain can, to a certain extent, determine her own agricultural policy. The balance of food supply has developed on the assumption that food imports can be paid for by exports of other goods: in view of problems of world food production, it might be prudent for more

[6]DHSS (1974) *Diet and Coronary Heart Disease* HMSO London.
[7]Thompson A.M. (1978) *Proceedings of the Nutrition Society*, 37, 3.

emphasis to be put on home food production.

Duckham (1975)[8] considered that Britain could increase food input by switching more to human food crops at the expense of animals, and could do this without prejudicing the level of human nutrition. However, once again, political considerations came into play, in that the implied changes in food habits may be seen to be unpopular. In 1975 a white paper entitled *Food from our own resources*[9] declared that domestic food production was to be increased to cut down the size of the import bill. The foods chosen for expansion were those that would yield the greatest economic return!

This kind of reasoning by governments is well illustrated by the case of school milk as described by Wardle in his book *Changing food habits in the United Kingdom*[10]. School milk was introduced in schools in 1934, and although there was some thought given to the nutritional implications of the measure, the main reason for its introduction was economic. Surplus milk was being wasted and milk prices were falling so that to supply milk to schools increased demand. The scheme was expanded during the war and by 1946, when various reports had confirmed the advantages of providing school milk it was decided to provide milk to all school children. In the 1950s, 80 per cent of school children were estimated to be taking school milk. However, in the late '60s and '70s, both Labour and Conservative governments decided to curtail school milk as an economy measure. It is now only available to children under 7 years and those who require it on medical grounds. No nutritional evidence was asked for, and the Committee that was set up by the Conservatives in 1971, has still to publish any results. The National Food Survey statistics show that a statistically significant decrease in milk consumption between 1970-72 occurred in lower income groups with one or two children. Now in 1980, there has been a suggestion by farmers that milk could be sold at a reduced rate to local authorities to provide milk for schools.

The EEC is shaping food choice in the United Kingdom by other means than shaping our agricultural policies, or subsidising some of our food. The Market attempts to remove barriers to trade that extend along national boundaries, and thus attempts have been made to standardise foods.

In Britain, sausages are made from meat and cereal, while sausages on the continent are mainly meat with a little amount of cereal. Ice cream in France, Germany, Denmark and Luxembourg, contains cream, whereas in Britain, Holland and Belgium it contains vegetable fats. As these differences can only be resolved by detailed talks, negotiations take a long time as nations cannot be persuaded to change their eating habits easily. So that despite the initial idea that food law should be uniform, it

[8]Duckham A.N. (1975) *Nutrition* 29, 6.
[9]MAFF (1975) *Food from our own resources* Cmnd 6020 HMSO London.
[10]Wardle C. (1977) *Changing food habits in the United Kingdom* Earth Resources Research.

would take too long to reach agreement. It was agreed that directives and legislation should only be drafted where this would assist inter-state trade. There are obviously various aspects of food legislation where uniformity is very desirable, such as additives, labelling and hygiene. There is a difference between directives and regulations. An EEC regulation is a proposal from the Commission which, having been approved by the Council of Ministers, immediately becomes law in all member states. For example, the grading of fresh fruit and vegetables is an EEC regulation. An EEC directive is a proposal from the Commission which, having been proposed by the Council of Members, is converted within a stated period into appropriate national legislation in each member state.

However, although the EEC has tried to standardise food, albeit unsuccessfully, it has as yet passed no laws to protect health, such as our *Food and Drugs Act* (see above), or the *Consumer Protection Act 1961* of the United Kingdom, which relates to the packaging of food stuffs.

Manufacturers

There is no doubt that food technology has brought about considerable changes in food availability, and also that manufacturers continue to exert strong influences on what the consumer eats.

The advent of processes such as canning, freezing and dehydration have had profound effects on the types of food available. The parallel development of more efficient transport systems has meant that a wide variety of food products is readily available to consumers all over the country.

In the past, the typical small community was in most respects self-contained, making use of local crops and animal products obtained in the locality. Food availability depended on season. (Aylward 1975)[11]. Now, there is no subsistence farming in Britain; even those who live on farms buy most of their food, and more important, the bulk of our population is urban, and has to be fed every day, although food production is rural, seasonal and somewhat unreliable. For this reason, argues Duckham, preservation, processing, storage, marketing and pricing machinery is essential. (Duckham 1975)[8].

Apart from the development of various technological processes, Aylward (1975)[11] points to other trends in the food industry which will affect food availability. Changes from batch to continuous processes, together with increased size and complexity of equipment result in an increased scale of operations, whereby products become widely available. There is also increased emphasis on the production of convenience foods, and the formation of mixed products and prepared

[11]Aylward F. (1975) *Nutrition* 29, 5.

meals. 'New foods' such as textured vegetable protein are also becoming more common.

Manufacturers may influence not only availability, but also nutritional standards of the diet. Over half the food consumed in the United Kingdom is processed or manufactured, and this indicates a responsibility of the industry to ensure the health and well-being of the population. (Rolfe 1980)[12]. However, Oddy (1976)[13] points out that the food technologist is likely to be far more concerned with quality and processing, leading to increased consumer demand, than with nutritive value.

Availability of foodstuffs to the consumer is thus the result of complex inter-actions, agricultural and commercial interests. In the next chapter, we consider the impact of economics on food choice.

[12]Rolfe E.J. (1980) *Food and Health* ed- Birch G.C., Parker K.T. Applied Science Publishers.
[13]Oddy D.J. (1976) *Proceedings of the Nutrition Society* 35, 139.

7: Economics and food choice

Within the universe of foods available to them, people can only choose what they can afford – or what they could afford if they changed the distribution of their income. It is often suggested that this is the key variable of all in influencing choice. Generally speaking, affluence is associated with a more adequate, varied and palatable diet, and changing food habits resulting from higher incomes are reflected in improved nutritional status. Improved, that is, if nutrient intakes are calculated as proportions of the *Recommended daily amount*; such values being higher for almost all nutrients amongst the better off. However, as previously demonstrated, affluence may bring its own nutritional problems associated with over-consumption – especially of sugar and animal fat.

In his early studies, Boyd Orr[1] demonstrated the effect of income on food choice: both the amount spent on food, and the types of commodities purchased varied with income. Whilst, as might be expected, absolute expenditure on food rose with income, as a proportion of total income it decreased. This is because there is obviously a limit to how much food can be consumed by an individual, or family. Foods which were bought more by higher income groups included meat and fish, dairy products, fruits and vegetables. People on lower incomes tended to use more condensed milk instead of fresh milk, and margarine instead of butter. Products such as potatoes, bread and flour did not appear to be markedly affected by income.

Much of this still holds true, though the proportion of disposable income spent on food has fallen from 27 per cent in 1938, to 19 per cent in 1977[2]. Expenditure still varies depending on income as does the nature of consumption patterns. Consideration of the findings of the National Food Survey indicate some of the ways in which prices affect food choice. For example, the removal of food subsidies during 1977 resulted in a reduced demand for the products affected, compared with non-subsidised items[3]. (Though this did not happen in the case of cheese.) Butter consumption increased temporarily after the introduction of the EEC subsidy. Other factors are at work, so that price and income have only a crude and limited effect[4]. Price increases are not always matched

[1]Orr B.J. (1936) *Food Health and Income* Macmillan Education, London.
[2]Angel L.J., Hurdle G.E., (1978) *Economic Trends* No. 294 CSO HMSO, London.
[3]MAFF (1978) *Household Food Consumption and Expenditure 1977* HMSO, London.
[4]McKenzie J. (1979) *Proceedings of the Nutrition Society* 38, 2.

by reductions in consumption, and conversely, stable prices do not necessarily lead to increased consumption. The nature of the commodity, and availability of substitutes or alternatives are important considerations. For example, price pressures probably affect meat consumption less than that of other foods. *Figure 7.1* shows long-term responses to price increases in different food commodities.

Figure 7.1 Price increases and food consumption 1957-72

	Price increase	Volume change
fish	+111%	− 4%
bread and cereals	+ 84%	− 8%
meat and bacon	+ 76%	+16%
sugar, preserves and confectionery	+ 69%	+ 4%
vegetables	+ 54%	+39%
oils and fats	+ 49%	+ 2%
dairy products	+ 46%	+28%
fruit	+ 46%	+21%
beverages	+ 27%	+33%
All food (household)	**+ 62%**	**+16%**

Adapted from King, S. (1979) (unpublished)

When income is restricted, it is not unlikely that the food budget will be reduced as it allows for more flexibility than, say, the rates, rent or gas bill, which are relatively fixed. Thus in times of economic hardship expenditure on food may be particularly curtailed. As unemployment levels rise, and many workers are faced with the prospect of redundancy, patterns of food consumption may be affected. When cutbacks are made, they are not necessarily based on nutritional considerations. Analysis of the surveys of William Nield, Mayor of Manchester in 1841, shows that families whose incomes were reduced by unemployment did not switch from meat to bread, but reduced consumption all round[5]. People tend to retain foods which are of emotional significance to them (see next chapter) at the expense of what is perhaps nutritionally more sound. Food costs bear little relationship to actual costs, or to nutritional quality. Cost is determined largely by what the consumer is willing to pay, and this in turn is a reflection of the 'status' or 'prestige' attached to a food. A food may be cheap and nutritionally excellent, eg milk, or expensive and nutritionally poor, ie confectionery.

Recent years have seen a decline in real income, and a shift in some

[5]Barker T.C. et al (1970) *The Dietary Surveys of Dr Edward Smith 1862-3* Staples Press, London.

food habits. Breakfasts are more often centred on cereal or toast, instead of egg, bacon and beans, whilst dishes like sausage and egg have been elevated to main meal status[6]. Convenience and time-saving may also be at work here, as may weight consciousness. This trend may indeed be viewed as a desirable one in view of current dietary concerns. Convenience foods are losing some of their popularity, leading to an increase in the purchase of raw ingredients for home baking and cooking, and there seems to be little doubt that expense is a factor here. There is some evidence that where money for food is strictly limited in the home, it is the father, then the children who have priority at meal times, with the mother most likely to go without[7]. In low income families, the diets of some members may be maintained at an adequate level at the expense of others. For this reason, studies concerned with relating household food intake and nutritional status, should look carefully at distribution patterns. Of course, good nutrition can be achieved on a relatively low income, though the resulting diet can be rather monotonous: this might result in insufficient food being consumed to meet energy needs.

'Even if we persuade people to adopt new patterns to maintain nutritional adequacy in time of hardship, if they cannot choose the foods they want they will still rightly consider themselves to be poor: they have been deprived'.[8]

Economic restrictions may particularly affect the nutrition of elderly people: as a group they tend to spend a higher percentage of their total outlay on the basic necessities of food, fuel and housing, and little is left over to allow for flexibility and variety. As well as having to juggle with a limited budget, elderly people may not be able to shop around so easily. Rehousing in estates on outskirts of towns may bring environmental advantages, but commonly food prices are higher than in the town centre, and regular journeys to town may be both impracticable and prohibitively expensive.

One way of assessing whether or not income affects food choice, is to ask people if and how they would change their buying habits if they had more money available. Meat, fruit, fish, milk and eggs are popular items which would be increased[9,10].

Occasionally, economic restrictions may bring nutritional benefits. A recent newspaper article[11] discusses the effects of financial stringencies on confectionery consumption. Children are being more careful of how they spend their pocket money. Manufacturers blame VAT, increased production costs, and reduced orders for the increases in their prices: . . .

[6]Stiles J., Cameron D. (1974) *Nutrition* 28, 1 p22.
[7]Land H. (1970) *Large Families in London* Bell.
[8]McKenzie J. (1974) *Proceedings of the Nutrition Society* 33, 67.
[9]McKenzie J. (1975) *Nutrition* 29, 5.
[10]Fieldhouse P. (1979) Unpublished.
[11]*Sunday Times* (1980) 15th June *Sticky Times for the Sweet Trade* p53.

'increased unemployment and a consequent drop in families' available cash is a further reason for sweets being left on the shelf'. However high prices must be a major reason for the drop in consumption.

Benefits

Various welfare benefits are available to people on low incomes, though they are not always taken up, either through ignorance of their existence, refusal to accept what is seen as 'charity', or simply because of the complexity of obtaining them. A Ministry of Social Services study in 1966[12] showed that over a third of children in families with a full-time earner did not receive the free school meals to which they were entitled. Families receiving supplementary benefit or family income supplement are entitled to free school meals for their children. Other low-paid workers are means-tested if they apply for this benefit – a procedure which is not acceptable to many people.

For pregnant and breast-feeding mothers and children under 5, free milk and vitamins are available, if income is below a set level[13]. Each person in the family who qualifies gets seven free pints of milk a week, or two free packets of baby milk, plus free children's vitamin drops and mothers' vitamin tablets. This also applies to handicapped children aged 5 to 16 years who are not attending school, whatever their parental income.

Selective benefits are not necessarily the best way to support those on low incomes. Land[14] decribes the problem of the 'poverty trap' whereby individuals, by earning a small amount of extra money lose as much or more in the value of means-tested benefits for which they become inelegible.

Whatever money people have available to spend on food, the way in which they spend it will depend on a range of social, cultural and psychological factors. This forms the basis of the next chapter.

[12]Ministry of Social Security (1967) *Circumstances of Families: Report of an Enquiry* HMSO London.
[13]DHSS (1980) Leaflet M11.
[14]Land H. (1974) *Proceedings of the Nutrition Society* 33, 39.

8: Psycho-social factors

Since ancient times man has been influenced by a variety of factors when choosing his food, in deciding how it is prepared or who is to eat what. Anthropologists study the food habits of primitive societies, and we can learn much from them about how our modern food habits have been formed. Margaret Mead defined food habits as 'the culturally standardised set of behaviours in regard to food manifested by individuals who have been reared within a given cultural tradition'. Thus behaviours are systematically inter-related with other behaviours in the same culture[1]. If this is so, then to understand food habits we must be aware of the social structures, culture and religions of the society in which we are studying the food habits.

Gifft et al[2] suggested that each culture has a value system which determines what people in that culture regard as fit for human consumption and what can be eaten by who. Food habits are not inherent, they are learned from parents, relatives or friends.

That food habits are passed down through generations is demonstrated very well in the United Kingdom by one particular prejudice. Horse meat is not considered acceptable for human consumption in the UK, although in other parts of the world it is eaten, notably France. If asked why they do not eat horsemeat most people say they find it detestable or barbaric. The taboo is thought to have originated when Pope Gregory III decided there ought to be some obvious distinction between Christians and Vandals. He instructed Boniface to forbid Christians to eat horsemeat, which previously both Vandals and Christians ate.

Differences in food preparation can be brought about by economic factors, religion, or the woman's role in that society. In the East women spend much of their day either preparing food or supervising its preparation. The elaborate dishes cannot be made in a small space of time as they involve the grinding of fresh spices and the preparation of numerous side dishes. Indeed in India each household will have its own special blend of curry powder and it is considered an important part of a girl's education to be able to produce the dishes her mother cooks. In the UK because of economic pressures and social change occurring during two world wars when women had to take over men's jobs, many women work outside the home. In 1974, half of all married women were in paid

[1] *The Problem of Changing Food Habits* (1944) National Council Bulletin 108 Committee on Food Habits. Washington D.C.
[2] Gifft H.H. et al (1972) *Nutrition Behaviour and Change*. Prentice Hall.

employment[3]. This means that working wives have less time to prepare meals and as convenience foods are available, these may be used as labour saving devices. Even if convenience foods are not used, meals are simpler than in the East and take less time to prepare.

Special properties either magical or medicinal have long been attributed to food, sometimes because of the colour or shape of the food item, Hypocrates the Greek physician regarded cabbage as having medicinal properties and recommended it to his patients for a variety of disorders.

In medieval times food was related to the humours, thus red meat was choleric and was thought to induce bad temper or violence. This idea persisted through to Charles Dickens' time, in Oliver Twist the Beadle suggested that Oliver is being difficult because he has been given meat.

Many primitive peoples believe that the characteristics possessed by a certain animal will be conferred on them if they eat meat from that animal. For example, the American Indians of the Kansas tribe believe that by eating the flesh of dogs they will become brave and faithful.

Folklore and myth still influence peoples ideas about food in the United Kingdom today. There are many examples of this, many elderly ladies believe port is good for anaemia, presumably because of its rich red colour. Brown eggs are preferred by many consumers to white as they believe they taste better and are more nutritious. Aphrodisiac properties are still ascribed to certain foods, usually exotic foods such as lotus flowers. Oysters and champagne are widely believed to make ladies more susceptible to the charms of lovers, perhaps the effect, if any, owes more to the intoxicating effect of the champagne than to any mysterious substance in either oysters or champagne.

The quantity of food consumed varies from one culture to another. Fatness is a desirable trait in some cultures, denoting wealth or an abundant supply of food; and children in these cultures are encouraged to eat as much as they can and not to leave anything. Hilda Bruch[4] gives the example of the immigrant, Jewish mothers of the 1930s in New York who implored their children to eat and become fat as they reasoned that a fat child could not have tuberculosis. This, in adulthood produced people who felt guilty if they did not overeat. In contrast, the Hindus see abstenance as a great virtue, hence Gandhi was much admired for his fasting, it being a sign of spiritual greatness.

Food may serve as a status symbol in society. Foods may have associations with class, fish and chips are considered by many people to be a lower class food, whereas dover sole and wine are considered upper class. Foreign foods may acquire a high status but this depends upon the esteem in which the race from which the food originates is held. Staple

[3] Social Trends 1974 CSO HMSO London.
[4] Bruch H. (1974) Eating Disorders, Obesity, Anorexia Nervosa and the Person Within Routledge and Kegan Paul, London.

foods may be held in high esteem, the Japanese prize rice very highly while the Scots regard oats in the form of porridge as their staple breakfast food.

Festivals and feasts may have their own special foods associated with them. In America at Thanksgiving turkey is eaten. Eggs are given at Easter in the UK, although they are not part of the Christian ritual, they are probably a sign of fertility dating from Pagan times.

Many social occasions or meetings involve eating or drinking, it may be that eating or drinking with a person establishes a bond, or implies trust. In some primitive tribes it was thought that the soul could escape from the body when a person was eating and so the mouth was shielded during eating, and meals were only taken within the family in case an enemy took possession of one's soul.

The idea that eating with people lower down in the hierarchy is unacceptable is common in the British society. Teaching hospitals segregate the consultants in their own dining room and have many eating places for the various grades of staff, the lowest being the canteen. Could it be that the higher grades in the hierarchy see themselves at risk if seen indulging in a human activity like eating, it may detract from their godlike status.

Religion

JUDAISM

Many of the Jewish food laws appear to be hygiene laws associated with life in a hot climate. This may not be strictly true, the law which forbids the eating of pig may have been made because the Jews were nomadic and pigs cannot be herded. However, the same law also forbids any animal that is cloven footed and does not chew the cud, eg camel. It is probably a coincidence that pigs were not a very safe food as they act as an intermediate host for tapeworm.

The laws relating to food are laid down in the Talmud, some of them can also be found in the Old Testament in Leviticus. Meat must be prepared according to traditional ritual and is said to be Kosher once this has been carried out. The ritual involves cutting the throat of the animal and letting the blood drain, the meat is then further prepared by the housewife by soaking and sprinkling it with salt.

Milk and meat are not allowed at the same meal and separate utensils are used for each. This involves considerable care as separate bowls must be used for washing the utensils used in preparing and cooking meat and milk dishes. As no work may be done on the Sabbath and this includes cooking, a method of slow cooking is used to supply the midday meal on Saturday, this is called the cholent.

The main Jewish festival is Passover, during which unleavened bread is eaten. The main fast is the Day of Atonement, when Jews are supposed to fast and pray. One interesting feature of Judaism is that wine is taken as part of the meal and drunk with other members of the family, and some sociologists believe that it is because of this that there is an extremely low rate of alcoholism among Jews.

ISLAM

The religion of Muslims, Islam, is in its dietary laws very similar to that of Judaism. The laws are laid down in the Koran and it is decreed that the flesh of cloven-footed animals, which do not chew the cud, cannot be eaten; very similar to the law in the Talmud. Muslims will not only shun any pig or pork product, they will avoid anything that has come into contact with pork products, such as meat in an English butchers which may have been cut with the same knife as pork. Strict Muslims require that their meat has been ritually slaughtered by being bled to death and dedicated to God by a Muslim, the meat is then known as Halal. However, some Muslims will accept Kosher meat as it has been slaughtered by similar means. In common with Jews, Muslims are forbidden to eat shellfish, but fish, provided it is alive when taken from the sea is permitted.

In a Muslim home, the men eat first and the wife and children eat later unseen by the man. This custom has been relaxed in many Muslim homes in the UK. In contrast to the Jewish faith, alcohol is forbidden.

The main fast for Muslims occurs at Ramadan and this may be particularly important in its effect on schoolchildren. The fast occurs at the ninth month of the lunar year and Muslims are expected neither to eat nor drink between dawn and sunset. In this country this could entail a thirteen-hour fast, since girls from the age of 12 years and boys from 15 years are expected to participate, this can lead to lack of concentration at school. Some people are excused, such as pregnant and lactating women, the incurably ill and the elderly. Menstruating women are excused but have to fast at another time.

HINDUISM

There are two main tenets in Hinduism, the sanctity of the cow and caste. Caste is the hereditary class within the community, although it is officially outlawed in India in practice it is very difficult for the lowest classes to improve their position and many are condemned to a miserable existence.

Orthodox Hindus believe in the doctrine of ahimsa (not killing) and this, together with the sanctity of the cow, forms the basis of their food habits. Hindus believe if they behave wrongly in this life they may be re-incarnated as an animal, they thus believe all life is related to them. Milk and milk products may be eaten because the animal life is not taken, in fact ghee (clarified butter) is said to sanctify food cooked in it.

Some Hindus will eat mutton, but fish is not much eaten and they prefer white fish to oily fish. Hindu women in particular have a revulsion for eggs, and will usually not even touch them, the men, however, will occasionally eat them. Hindu children at school will usually only eat the vegetables as they are unsure as to the origin of the other foods. Unfortunately, not all schools provide a vegetarian diet. Fasting or abstention is regarded as a great virtue among Hindus and some spend two or three days a week fasting. Food is closely associated with religious ceremonies and at a Hindu wedding ceremony the bride and groom feed each other with sweetmeats.

SIKHISM

This is a comparatively recent religion, being founded some 600 years ago by Guru Nanak. Sikhs are easily recognised in that their menfolk wear turbans and grow beards.

Sikhs are forbidden to eat beef but may eat pork. Their meat should be killed by a blow to the head of the animal. Sikhs are much more liberal in their views on eating and adapt much easier to new lifestyles than do Muslims or Hindus. Very few are vegetarians and although they are not expected to take alcohol, many do.

Psychological influences

Food produces an emotional response in all people, but since everyone is an individual with different experiences the responses will vary from person to person, and so individual food habits will be produced. Babies learn to associate food with relief of hunger and bodily contact. How a child learns about food affects his later eating patterns and his behaviour with regard to food.

If a child is coaxed or bribed as a toddler to eat, then later in childhood he may use refusal of food as a means of getting his own way. Introducing a child to a wide variety of flavours and textures is less likely to result in an adult with very restricted food habits who is unwilling to try any new food.

Most of us are aware that food can be used to substitute for expressing our real feelings, maybe of depression or frustration. The thought 'I have had a bad day so I will cheer myself up by having a chocolate/cake/ biscuits' must have crossed most of our minds at some time. Students taking exams usually admit to having different meal patterns and food habits at this time of stress. The most common change that occurs is that intake of hot liquids especially stimulants such as tea and coffee increases. Eating can be used as a substitute for love, some food is closely associated with love from babyhood, deprived children and later adults may use food to comfort themselves and make up for a lack of love.

Familiarity with a food often makes it more acceptable, perhaps initially in primitive man this was a protective device to guard against poisoning. Toddlers much prefer familiar food when they are in strange surroundings, perhaps it gives a feeling of security. Immigrants of many different cultures may use familiar food as a means of feeling secure and not losing their identity in a foreign land. In the United Kingdom Asians and West Indians in particular have their own food stores and are willing to spend more money on familiar foods which may have to be specially imported, and thus are more expensive than the traditional foods available in the UK.

Familiarity with food and whether it is chosen or not also extends to its presentation. Bread is a familiar food product, but if it is presented to consumers dyed blue, green or red they then become unwilling to buy it or taste it.

Food may be associated with memories – either good or bad. If the memory is a happy one then that food may be desirable, if the memory is bad then the food will be disliked. These likes and dislikes, particularly the latter, may be so firmly fixed that it is impossible to overcome them unless the memory of why we dislike the food can be recalled and even then it may prove impossible.

Therapeutic requirements obviously play an important part in some peoples food habits. Diabetics need to conform to a meal pattern which has been agreed with the dietitian. Although this meal pattern will have been tailored to the patients requirements, both therapeutic and social, there will be little opportunity for impulse. How many of us eat impulsively either through boredom or social requirements? We do not often consider it, but the diabetic must always consider it. There are other therapeutic diets which are much more restrictive than a diabetic diet and these may impose some restrictions not only on the patient but also the family. In families where a child is on a special diet, some mothers find that they feel so guilty about depriving the child of foods which he likes, that they impose the restriction on the whole family.

People living in institutions are obviously reliant on the caterers in the institution for what they have and when they have it. Some institutions are notoriously restrictive which may be due to lack of staff or imaginations. Psychiatric hospitals may rely on monotonous menus and sloppy food because they may feel that the inmates do not care about what they eat, and they have little to spend on food.

The effect of changing meal patterns can produce interesting effects on people. When people are admitted to acute hospitals, once they feel better find that they are constantly thinking of food, and when the next meal is coming, even though they are often being given more than they eat at home.

Members of the armed forces may become so used to having meals prepared and given at certain times that when they become civilians, they find it extremely difficult to adjust.

Food fads

There seems to have been over the past decade, an upsurge in the number of food fads. Many people in the pursuit of health rather than exert any discipline over themselves in eating or exercising actually prefer to believe that eating one certain food or taking one food supplement will supply the answer to their problems. Manufacturers and promoters of these products are only too aware of this, and they exploit it and use scientific fact, quoted out of context, to impress the consumer.

The range of foods and other products is wide; from honey, a food we have been using for thousands of years, to trace elements the importance of which is now being recognised, but not in the quantities suggested by some health food fanatics.

These products are not only promoted by the firms selling them, but the public are subjected to admonitions from well known celebrities who claim the foods can do many things, all of which are highly desirable; prevent ageing, help reduce weight, relieve arthritis. Some celebrities even sell the substances which they are so fond of telling the public are good for them.

Currently, if we look on the shelves in chemists shops and health food shops, we can see an amazing range of products. Lecithin appears to be in vogue at the moment as the panacea for all ills. Cider vinegar and kelp are the main adjuncts for slimming, kelp no doubt is supposed to stimulate the thyroid gland because of its iodine content and boost metabolism. Cider vinegar is more difficult to explain, maybe it tastes so unpleasant it puts people off eating!

Affluence in some cases means that people are prepared to spend large amounts of money on special foods which promise slimness, good health or sexual potency. Recently a product came to our attention which was being sold at a well known ladies hairdressers. It was a slimming package which cost £30 for a five day supply and promised a marvellous weight loss. The package in fact contained a bottle of vitamin tablets, a bottle of cider vinegar and kelp tablets, ginseng, and some soya granules. Instructions were also given to limit fluid intake to 16 oz for three days, the marvellous weight loss would no doubt be due to dehydration. This whole package could probably be assembled for £2, and while perhaps those foolish enough to believe it deserved to be gulled, the instructions and advice were dangerous.

So far we have discussed food fads that are silly but not (apart from the above product) dangerous. There are, however, some products advertised that may indeed be harmful. Some pop magazines advertise substances to give a lift or help people to 'freak out'. Some of these, such as mandrake root, do in fact contain harmful substances.

Food cultism

One of the most widespread food cults in the western world particularly America and the United Kingdom is the slimming cult. Medical opinion about the dangers of obesity could have been ignored had it not suddenly become fashionable to be very slim. Twiggy in the 1960s became the idol of many young women who aspired to be of the same proportions. This fashion in turn produced the commercial slimming clubs, of which there are now a multitude ranging from the international down to the local.

Although most slimming clubs imply they are there to help the obese, their primary concern is financial. They safeguard their interests by suggesting that members ought to get their doctor's permission before starting on the diet, but do not run any health checks while members are attending the club and following the diet. Many general practitioners are in total ignorance of what advice is being given to their patients or how little training (two weeks at the most) the group leaders have. Their main qualification is that they have lost weight, but how relevant is that, we do not demand that our appendix is taken out by someone who has had theirs removed but is not medically qualified.

These clubs claim wonderful success but what do they mean by success? Usually dramatic short-term weight loss, with the slimmer returning again and again to the club, to be slimmed down again and again. This does of course mean a constant source of income for the club.

Many methods used by these clubs are potentially hazardous. One organisation recommends using behavioural techniques and teaches them to their leaders! Put this together with a very strict diet which even forbids certain foods at certain times of the day, and it could be the recipe for misfortune.

Group therapy works with many slimmers and ought to be left in the hands of those who are qualified to do it.

Since the 1960s the influence of the East on food cults has grown. Those particularly susceptible to this influence are those who are anti-establishment, seeking some meaning to life, or those who have 'dropped out'. The most dangerous cult to come from the Orient is that of the Zen Macrobiotic diet. This was created by Georges Ohsawa, a Japanese author, who claims to be a philosopher and scientist. The diet, he says, will lead to Nirvana, a state of ultimate happiness, and it can cure all ills, improve memory and expansion of free thinking[5]. The diet is based on a series of dietary regimes. Gradually all foods except brown rice are eliminated. At first, animal foods are omitted, then fruit and cereals and finally vegetables, this last stage is called stage 7. Food must be chewed thoroughly and fluid intake is restricted. This diet is known to have brought about the deaths of some young people in the USA who followed

[5]Stare J. (1970) *Food Cultism and Nutritional Quackery*. Symposium of the Swedish Nutrition Foundation p.51 Almquist and Wiksell. Stockholm.

the diet strictly through to the final level. There have also been several cases reported of the children of followers of the cult being admitted to hospital suffering from dehydration.

In the UK in 1979 an article in the British Medical Journal[6] reported the admission to hospital of four children suffering from the effects of their parents giving them a macrobiotic diet. All the children were under developed physically and mentally. Some showed signs of kwashiorkor, rickets and other nutritional deficiencies. The parents proved very resistant to advice about diet, but eventually were persuaded to allow the children to follow a more liberal vegetarian diet. Thus food fads or cults followed by parents can have a pronounced effect on the children.

[6]Roberts I.F. et al (1979) *British Medical Journal* 1, p296-298.

SECTION IV
Shaping food choice

9: How food habits are formed

Food habits are characteristic and repetitive acts performed under the impetus of the need to provide nourishment and meet social and emotional goals[1]. Children are highly dependent on others for their food intake in the early years, and many of the patterns of eating seen in adult life are established at this time.

The acquisition of food habits may be seen in terms of socialisation processes. Socialisation is a concept embracing the actions of imparting culturally valued norms: more specifically, knowledge, values, attitudes and routines considered worthwhile by a community or society[2]. It operates in different ways throughout the lifespan, as illustrated in *Figure 9.1.*

Primary socialisation occurs in the early childhood years mainly through the influence of the parents and of other close relatives and friends. In nutritional matters, the strongest influence is likely to be that of the mother, who is usually most intimately involved with food preparation and presentation. Transmission of norms and internalisation of routines occurs at this time, as the child identifies with the parents' behaviour. Processes of reinforcement, modelling and imitation result in new behaviours being adopted and integrated with previous experience.

Appropriate, or desired behaviour is sanctioned: thus the deviant or undesired behaviour is encouraged: thus the child learns through a system of reward and punishment. Foods begin to take on emotional significance for the child, which may well override their nutritional value. Sweet foods, particularly, may be used as gifts, treats and tokens of affection, as well as rewards and bribes[3].

[1]Gifft H.H. et al (1972) *Nutrition Behaviour and Change* Prentice-Hall.
[2]Tones B.K. (1978) *Effectiveness and Efficiency in Health Education: a review of theory and practice* SHEU Edinburgh.
[3]MacArthur C. (1975) *MSc thesis* Manchester.

Figure 9.1 A nutrition career

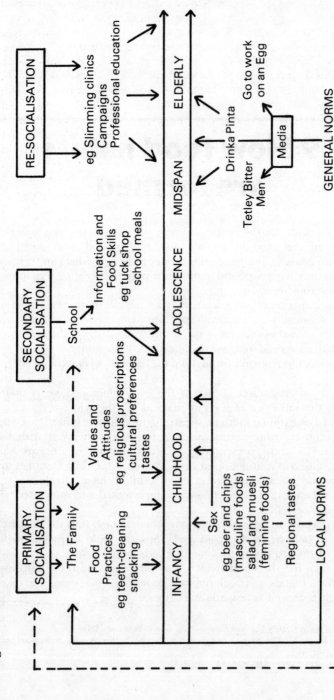

Source: Tones, BK (unpublished)

Sweetness may become associated with goodness. The habit of eating sweet foods, once acquired in childhood, persists into adult life, and has obvious implications for nutritional health. Avoidance of sweet foods, such as cakes, biscuits and confectionery in, for example, an energy-controlled diet, is still viewed as a sort of punishment and frustrated reducers still guiltily 'treat' themselves to illicit cream cakes. A child brought up without added sugar and with restriction of sweets is not being deprived, and a good foundation is being laid for future health. Similarly, children who are exposed to a wide variety of foods in early life are less likely to become faddy about their diets, and more willing to try new tastes and non-traditional dishes. This may be very important, not only in adding interest to the diet, but also in allowing more flexibility during times of retricted food availability. It is wrong to assume that children have the same taste preferences as adults, though if they see that Mum will never eat carrots and Dad always has two spoonfuls of sugar in tea, they are more likely to develop similar patterns themselves. The practice of sweetening or salting food to suit adult preference should be strictly avoided in childhood.

In addition to the acquisition of routines and habits during primary socialisation, the period of secondary or formal socialisation is very important. This is when knowledge is acquired which is necessary for a rational explanation of behaviour and which serves as a reinforcement for the maintenance of behaviour. Characteristically, secondary socialisation occurs in a more formal context than does primary socialisation, and the main agency involved is the school. The child is exposed to a wider range of influences and to constantly differing values and opinions.

Environmental experiences are important, in that, tuck shops and school meals set examples, and as they operate within an educational setting may be seen as representing what is acceptable nutritionally. Too often 'good nutrition' is rejected because it is represented by an unattractive, poorly prepared meal – though of course some school catering standards are excellent. And who can blame children for rejecting the message that sweets are harmful to health, when they are actually put up for sale in the school building?

Socialisation which is nutritionally orientated can be enhanced by the provision of sound nutritional education in schools, and this is an issue which is taken up in chapter 11.

As individuals we frequently adopt the values, attitudes and behaviours of social groups to which we would like to belong. This process is referred to as anticipating socialisation[2]. If children adopt values and behaviours in anticipation of future roles (eg adolescent girls adopting the norm of slimness) it could be one of the school's functions to provide anticipatory guidance.

Socialised health behaviour may either involve a decision-making component or be routine. Routines are habitualised forms of behaviour characterised by their economy of effect, predictability and absence of the need for decision. If these routines fail to maintain a state of health, a person will have to make a decision concerning his health behaviour.

Educational effort must then be directed towards promoting favourable decisions: with routines, educational effort is unnecessary and, to this extent, socialising a routine health behaviour or practice would seem to be desirable. However, if the routine fails or becomes inappropriate, decision-making skills, hitherto bypassed, will be needed.

Both local and general norms will have an influence on food habits in a society, whilst their influence on very young children is an indirect one, it becomes more direct as the child gets older. Certain practices are seen to be acceptable or unacceptable in cultural or social terms, whilst others are promoted, mainly through the mass media, as being eminently desirable. The conflicts which arise during socialisation are indicated by the part-title of a useful paper by Leo Baric[4] *Social expectations vs. personal preference* . . .' in which ways of influencing health behaviour are discussed.

Advertising

Hanssen[5] says of advertising that it . . . 'persuades us that the right taste for a food is the result of some particular concept designed by marketing men, created by food technologists and produced in beautiful factories with sales potential as the guiding light rather than nutritional consequences'.

Thompson[6] highlights the profit motive behind much food production by drawing attention to the enormous sums of money spent on market research and advertising designed to alter food habits. In view of this it is reasonable to claim that manufacturers are more interested in creating new consumer demands than in meeting existing ones.

The main objective of food advertising is to promote brands of food, rather than actual foods. The exceptions to this are various groups of food manufacturers formed into boards, bureaux or councils who are interested in increasing the consumption of a certain food. Examples are: the Butter Information Council, the Cheese Bureau, the Flour Advisory Bureau.

Advertising has its proponents and opponents, those in favour claim that it stimulates competition and brings prices down. Those against maintain that huge sums are spent on advertising promotions and these inevitably increase the price of the products. The amount spent on advertising food does not reflect the consumption of the food. Wardle[7]

[4]Baric L. (1976) *Journal Institute Health Education* 15, 3.
[5]Hanssen M. (1980) *Food and Health* ed- Birch G.C.,Parker K.T. Applied Science Publishers.
[6]Thompson A.M. (1978) *Proceedings of the Nutrition Society* 37, 3.
[7]Wardle C. (1977) *Changing Food Habits in the United Kingdom* Earth Resources Research.

gives the example of the amount spent on advertising breakfast cereals in 1973 being thirty times greater than that spent on sugar; but the retail sales of sugar are three times that of breakfast cereals. Products which sell well require little advertising, so that maybe trends in consumption can be observed by watching advertisements.

Nutritionists have a right to be concerned about advertising because some of the ways in which food is advertised are questionable giving a status to foods in order to promote them. Again some advertisements are actually misleading about the nutritional value of food. The advertising of the 'low carbohydrate' lagers is a good example of how the public can be misled by what is not said rather than what is said. One advertisement shows men drinking one of these lagers and while the words low carbohydrate are used, the men pat their midriffs, the implication being that they are slimming. What is not said is that because the alcohol content of this lager is higher it has the same or slightly higher energy value than normal lager.

Although there is no single piece of legislation that covers food advertisements, there are two pieces of legislation which have a direct bearing on food advertising, they are the *Food and Drugs Act 1955* and the *Food Labelling Regulations 1970*. *The Food and Drugs Act* contains not only provisions for prosecution of anyone who advertises food which is contaminated or adulterated, but also for prosecution of anyone who falsely describes a food or misleads as to its constituents. However, clever advertising as illustrated above, can easily bypass these requirements.

The *Food Labelling Regulations 1970* go further than the *Food and Drugs Act* in that it makes clear instructions as to what may and may not be said on a label about a food. Under this Act, slimming products and other special products such as food supplements are much more closely restrained from making false claims.

The Ministry of Agriculture, Fisheries and Food after consideration of recommendations by the Medical Research Council has put forward a suggested Code of Practice which would in essence mean that claims cannot be made about vitamins and minerals unless the amount present in the food conforms to a set of standards. Such as: 'unless the amount of food ordinarily consumed in one day contain at least one sixth of the daily requirement of the vitamin or mineral then,
a) no claim based on its presence should be made and
b) no reference to its presence is justified in any advertisements for the general public, or on any label.'

There are various bodies, professional and otherwise, which lay down codes of conduct for advertising, these bodies, however, lack any power to enforce these codes. The British Code of Advertising Practice[8] states that the advertising of alcoholic drinks should not exploit the immature, young, socially insecure or those with physical, mental or social

[8]*British Code of Advertising Practice* Advertising Standards Authority.

incapacity. It does believe it is proper for advertisements for alcoholic drinks to indicate that they give pleasure to many, are of high quality and are widely enjoyed in all classes of society. It is also acceptable to seek to persuade people to change brands or give information on products.

The Code also states that young people should not be encouraged to drink or start drinking, children ought not to be shown on advertisements for alcohol, nor may the advertisement put out a challenge. These provisions are in no way enforceable and merely act as guide lines.

The largest proportion of money spent on advertising food is allocated to television advertising. Since the early days of advertising, when it was merely stated that a product was better or cheaper than its competitors, advertising has become much more complex, relying on experts, like psychologists, to promote products by more devious means.

Fashion in advertising, even for food products, changes. In the late '70s and now into the '80s the theme of back to nature has been very much in evidence. An advertisement for frozen beans shows a plough pulled by two horses giving the impression of traditional farming methods being used in the production of the beans, as this is thought to make them more acceptable. In reality, of course, the whole process is highly mechanised.

The advertisements for a brown bread impress on us, in a wave of nostalgia, how the bread is the same as it was years ago, the implication being that it must be good if our grandparents ate it.

One interesting point about food advertising is that frozen food must be advertised so that a suggestion is made for the housewife to make her own contribution to the meal. Otherwise, she is not interested. Nor do women like to be told about cooking by a man[9].

The image of the perfect mother is used to sell food that is considered suitable for children, such as baked beans. In a recent advertisement the perfect mother instead of being annoyed with her children who have been playing near a ditch and fallen in merely dispatches them upstairs to wash, promising in honeyed tones to keep their beans warm!

Another advertisement used to imply that the perfect mother would never give her children anything but butter, how could she?

Many people maintain that the viewing public is not so gullible as the promoters believe. Although it is difficult to find out what effects these advertisements do have on food choice (manufacturers keep these facts a closely guarded secret) it is reasonable to assume that they must have the desired effect to a large extent as otherwise food manufacturers just would not bother.

[9]Williams C. (1976) *The Packaging of Women* Women in Media.

10: Changing food habits

Once values, attitudes and routines have been established, any attempt to change them may be referred to as resocialisation: it is with this process that nutrition education is frequently concerned. The law of primacy states that earlier influences are more powerful and long-lasting than later ones, and the marked lack of success in persuading people to alter their dietary habits illustrates this precisely. Even when modifications are required for specific therapeutic reasons they are not always carried out.

Although it is easy to believe that nutrition is concerned with persuading people to act in their own best interests, it is not always clear what those best interests are, and there are dangers of middle-class educators imposing their own values on other groups. For this reason, one school of thought saw that any form of health education should confine itself to providing facts, so that the individual has a rational basis for making his own decisions. However, it is well-known that mere provision of information is no guarantee that behaviour change will ensue, even if the information is accepted and comprehended. The Schools Council[1] were of the opinion that

'. . . there is a need not only to provide children with the information that they will need to make health decisions, but equally important to put them through a positive process of decision-making in order to prepare them for later, vital decisions'.

Persuasive communication

In the process of communication, several variables can be identified, whose interaction determines the outcome of the communication. The sender (source), the message and the recipient (audience) can all, to some extent be controlled, and manipulation of these variables may assist in promoting change.

Source variables are characteristics associated with the communicator, such as his credibility, expertise, trustworthiness, attractiveness, sincerity, status, etc. These may influence the receiver's confidence in the message, and thus affect the probability of its acceptance. Communication must be matched to the knowledge, social background, interests, purposes and needs of the recipient[2], and it is thus

[1]Schools Council (1977) *Health Education Project 5-13 years*. Thomas Nelson.
[2]Fletcher, C.M. (1973) *Communication in Medicine*. Roch Carling. Monograph.

vital to consider fully, audience characteristics. Audience variables include age, sex, intelligence, self-esteem, interests, personality, as well as previous relevant knowledge and attitudes.

Message variables include order of presentation, validity of arguments, emotional or rational content, high or low fear arousal, and clarity.

The factors described above are interactive: eg an emotive argument might lower the communicators perceived credibility. It is difficult therefore to study these factors in isolation and to quantify their individual effects.

Fishbein and Ajzen[3] suggest that discrepancy is an important variable. That is, the greater the initial difference between the view of the communicator and the view of the receiver, the less chance there is of the acceptance of the message. The amount of discrepancy can be influenced by the facilitating factors mentioned above. Its effects can be minimised when the communicator is highly credible and the receiver has initial low confidence in his own beliefs, and maximised when the receiver is strongly confident in his own initial beliefs, and the communicator is of low credibiity. Thus attempts at improving the likelihood of acceptance of a message involve increasing the level of facilitating factors.

An example of the effects of message variables is the use of fear-arousal. According to Janis and Festbach[4], implicit in the use of fear appeals is the assumption that when emotional tension is aroused, the audience will become more highly motivated to accept the reasoning beliefs or recommendations advocated by the communicator. However, this approach has several disadvantages, and it is probably not appropriate for use in nutrition education.

Knowledge and attitudes

One of the audience variables mentioned above referred to previous relevant knowlege. If we are to influence food habits at all, we need to be aware of what people already know and think about nutriton, so as to be able to devise appropriate educational strategies and messages.

There have been several studies over a number of years, concerned with the level of nutritional knowledge amongst the general public, and it is generally found that younger women from higher socio-economic groups are the most knowledgeable.

McKenzie[5] found that amongst issues of concern were included 'wholesomeness' or 'naturalness' of food, balance in the diet, specific links between food and disease, and achievement of an 'ideal' diet.

[3] Fishbein, M., Ajzen, I. (1975) *Belief, Attitude, Intention and Behaviour*. Addison-Wesley. Reading.
[4] Janis J.L. and Festbach S. (1963) *Journal of Abstracts in Social Psychology* 48, 79-92.
[5] McKenzie J. (1979) *Proceedings of the Nutrition Society* 38, 2.

Variety in the diet was associated with healthy eating, and together with modification, this could be a key point in nutrition education. Some foods or food groups were associated with specific diseases. For example, fatty foods were implicated in the causation of heart disease. People have become more familiar with the terms 'cholesterol' and 'polyunsaturated fatty acid' and there is some evidence that they do attempt to substitute 'vegetable' fats for 'animal' fats, eg using margarine instead of butter[6].

Overconsumption of sugary and starchy foods is seen to be potentially harmful to health, especially in leading to obesity. Cakes, biscuits and potatoes are cited as the main culprits, though bread is viewed with more ambivalence – there being some awareness of its wider food value.

In the surveys cited, excess use of processed foods was condemned, mainly through concern over the use of additives. 'Natural' foods received much verbal support, though as McKenzie said . . . 'people can quite happily disclaim on the merits of a natural diet whilst eating a convenience meal, heavily processed and containing many additives'.

This is a good illustration that even positive attitudes are not necessarily translated into action. Consumers claim to be confused by the contradictory messages presented to them, and the fact that 'the experts can't make up their minds'. This leads many to follow any 'new' advice, whatever the source (especially in the area of dieting) or else to reject all advice, on the grounds that it will probably change tomorrow!

A general high level of awareness of individual nutrients is apparent, but there is much confusion in relating nutrients to particular foodsuffs, and identifying nutrient functions. However, as Thomas[7] points out, this is not an entirely appropriate way of assessing nutritional knowledge, for whilst particular nutrients may not be associated with particular functions, the foods which contain those nutrients often are, eg milk is more readily associated with 'body-building' than is protein.

Some misconceptions remain, and may be fairly widespread. One example is that vitamin C is often associated with the prevention of the common cold, and similar ailments. Consumption of large amounts of vitamin C thus contributes to the achievement of the desired 'optimal diet' as described by McKenzie.

The heavy advertising of products with added vitamin C, and the implications of their benefits for health must be largely responsible for this situation. Certainly, there is no scientific justification for such claims[8].

In group discussions, held as part of the BMRB survey[6], emphasis was put on the opportunities for better feeding today. Many housewives felt that they had sounder ideas on family feeding than did their parents, and

[6]British Market Research Bureau (1973) *Food and Nutrition: report on a survey of housewives knowledge and attitudes.*
[7]Thomas, J.E. (1979) *1st Conference of the British Nutrition Foundation.* London.
[8]Taft G., Fieldhouse P. (1978) *Public Health* 92, 19-25.

that they were concerned with trying to improve the family diet. Changes desired were relatively minor, but included the increased use of meat and fruit. An interest in food values and balanced diets is expected of young mothers, but although they are becoming more aware of the importance of nutrition, they are generally disinterested in nutritional detail.

There is some evidence that increased nutritional knowledge is associated with better dietary practices, though overall educational attainment may be more influencial than nutritional knowledge *per se*. The relationship between changing knowledge and changing eating habits is complex, and many educational programmes, whilst succeeding in changing nutritional knowledge, have failed in effecting any change in actual dietary practice.

Attitude change

One of the first tasks then, in attempting to change food habits is to provide knowledge, and correct misconceptions. This leads on to a consideration of attitude change, and subsequent behaviour change.

Health belief models devised to help explain individual behaviours regarding health decisions suggest that before any action will be taken, an individual must:

1) see that his current behaviour poses a health threat to him
2) see this threat as being serious
3) see that effective measures are available to relieve the threat
4) see that the action involved is not disadvantageous to him.

In addition, there must be a 'trigger' or stimulus to action. An individual will only change his behaviour if he expects it to be beneficial to do so, and people learn to perform behaviours whch are expected to lead to positive gains. Fishbein[9] suggests that the belief set of an individual regarding the consequences of a particular behaviour (ie expectations) determine his attitude towards performing that particular behaviour. Attitudes are themselves precursors of intentions to indulge in a behaviour, and intention is translated into action with the provision of a suitable stimulus (*Figure 10.1*).

Using the example of breast-feeding, *Figures 10.2* and *10.3* show that certain beliefs are commensurate with breast feeding, whilst others are not. If beliefs from *Table 10.1* could be created or made more satient at the expense of beliefs in *Table 10.2* there should be a greater motivation to breast-feed.

In order to progress from intention to behaviour, certain enabling factors must be present[2]. These may include a favourable and supportive

[9]Fishbein M. (1976) 'Persuasive Communication' in *Communication between Doctors and Patients* ed- Bennett A.E., Oxford University Press for Nuffield Provincial Hospitals Trust.

environment and the possession of appropriate knowledge and skills. In our example, the mother must be confident in her own ability and skills in breast-feeding: she should be in a non-stressful environment where she receives practical support and encouragement, so that certain physiological events can occur successfully.

Studies have shown that special efforts to give support and encouragement have had short-term success – but breast-feeding has often been discontinued on discharge from hospital. Perhaps mothers felt that they must 'make an effort' whilst in hospital, but reverted to their 'own choice' of behaviour as soon as possible. If this is the case, educational effort should be directed at influencing this 'own choice' by creating or reinforcing beliefs leading to a favourable attitude to breast-feeding.

Table 10.1 Reasons for breast-feeding

It is the natural way
It is better for the baby's health
It makes the baby closer to you
Breast feeding is easier
Breast feeding is enjoyable
My husband wanted me to
I was advised to by the midwife
A friend told me breast-feeding was best
My mother breast fed me

Table 10.2 Reasons for not breast-feeding

Embarrassment
Not capable of breast-feeding
Breast feeding is repulsive
Not sufficient milk to breast-feed
Not able to see how much milk baby is getting
Fear of losing figure
Misinformation about breast-feeding
Restriction on social life
Because of other children
Because of other bad experiences
My husband did not want me to

Figure 10.1 Conceptual framework for the prediction of specific intentions and behaviours

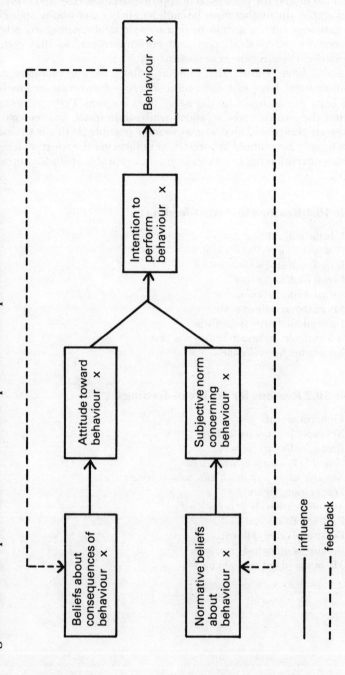

Fishbein M., Ajzen I. (1975) *Belief, Attitude, Intention and Behaviour* Addison-Wesley.

Figure 10.2 Beliefs leading to the establishment of bottle feeding

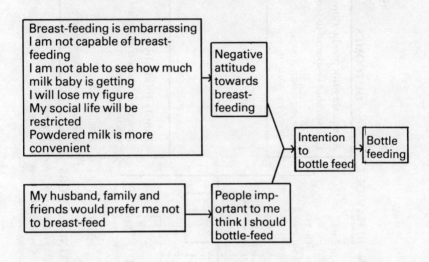

Figure 10.3 Beliefs leading to the establishment of breast-feeding

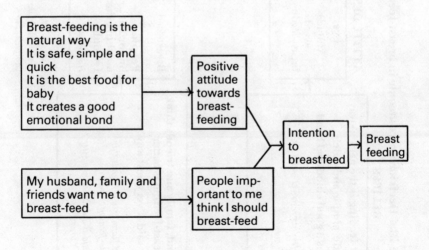

Figure 10.4 Decision and outcome in breast-feeding

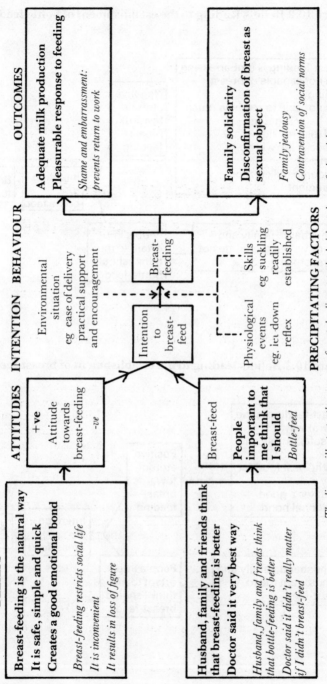

BELIEFS ATTITUDES INTENTION BEHAVIOUR OUTCOMES

Breast-feeding is the natural way
It is safe, simple and quick
Creates a good emotional bond

Breast-feeding restricts social life
It is inconvenient
It results in loss of figure

+ve
Attitude
towards
breast-feeding
-ve

Breast-feed
**People
important to
me think that
I should**
Bottle-fed

**Husband, family and friends think
that breast-feeding is better**
Doctor said it very best way

*Husband, family and friends think
that bottle-feeding is better*
*Doctor said it didn't really matter
if I didn't breast-feed*

Intention
to
breast-
feed

Environmental
situation
eg. ease of delivery
practical support
and encouragement

Physiological
events
eg. ict-down
reflex

Breast-
feeding

Skills
eg. suckling
readily
established

PRECIPITATING FACTORS

Adequate milk production
Pleasurable response to feeding

*Shame and embarrassment:
prevents return to work*

Family solidarity
**Disconfirmation of breast as
sexual object**

Family jealousy
Contravention of social norms

The diagram illustrates the sequence of events leading up to the decision to breast-feed, and the consequences of that decision. Some of the positive influences and outcomes are shown in bold type, whilst examples of negative influences and outcomes are shown in italics.

86

SECTION V
Approaches to nutrition education

II: Health and nutrition education

Health education

According to the World Health Organisation Expert Committee on Health Education[1] the aims of health education are:

1. To make health a valued community asset.
2. To equip people with the skills and knowledge that they can use to solve their own health problems.
3. To promote the development of health services.

If health education is viewed as the process of persuading people to act in their own best interests, it is apparent that it has been long established in an informal, unstructured way, often being embodied in traditional folklore. Whilst the emphasis laid upon health education remains centred on non-academic achievement, its theoretical concepts and methodology have developed in a more sophisticated way. A later definition from WHO emphasises the people orientation of health education[2].

> 'the focus of health education is on people and action. In general its aims are to persuade people to adopt and sustain health services available to them, and to take their own decisions, both individually and collectively to improve their health status and environment'.

Health education can act at the level of primary, secondary or tertiary prevention.

Primary prevention is concerned with promoting behaviours which are conducive to good health, and is aimed at a healthy population. Thus it includes the establishment of healthy food practices during childhood,

[1]World Health Organisation (1954) *Technical Report Series No. 89.*
[2]World Health Organisation (1969) *Technical Report Series No. 409.*

in order to avoid nutritional disorders in later life.

It may also directly attack the cause of a disease: eg by encouraging lime-soaking treatment of maize to prevent pellagra, or teaching hygienic methods of bottle-feed preparation to prevent gastro-enteritis.

Secondary prevention seeks to identify disease before symptoms appear, whilst intervention can still change the course of the disease, eg screening for phenylketonuria. There is still the possibility of stopping progression of the disease.

Tertiary prevention occurs when an individual has a disease but treatment prevents or minimises the damage to future health. An example would be the use of diet to control clinical diabetes.

The dilemma of the health educator lies in deciding how far to go in trying to influence people: whether to present the facts so that each individual can make his own informed decision, or to actively persuade people to adopt new health values. Certainly there is evidence that the mere acquisition of knowledge will not automatically lead to changes in attitudes and behaviour, even if the information is accepted and comprehended.

The Cohen Committee report, which provided the basis for health education in the United Kingdom was certainly of the opinion that health education must do more than provide information:

> '. . . it must also seek to influence people to act on the advice and information given, and must seek to counter pressures which are inimical to health'.[3]

Anderson[4] identifies health education as the essential communicational component of preventative medicine. However, it may be more broadly viewed in the context of stimulating awareness and discussion of social and political issues as they affect health. The Politics of Health Group offer such an approach to nutrition education in their pamphlet *Food and Profit*.

Anderson illustrates how a range of techniques and activities can contribute to health education:

> '. . . Health education is done by teaching about health in schools and by using that battery of communication methods and techniques associated with face-to-face text-based teaching. Health education is done by distance-learning methods: by television commercials, by posters, by telephone advice services. It is done by informal and non-directive work, by the organisation or support of self-help and community groups, by families and peer groups. It is done incidentally when doctors and nurses talk to patients: when environmental health officers administer the law. It is done indirectly by pressure groups lobbying for legal or organisational or fiscal

[3]Central and Scottish Health Services Council (1964) *Health Education* HMSO London.
[4]Anderson D.C. (1979) *Health Education in Practice* Croom Helm London.

changes. . . . It is done by parental and sibling example and care in the family: by neighbourly information and support in the garden and pub . . .'

Nutrition education

Within the extensive field of health education, the role of nutrition education is of particular importance. There is an intimate relationship between our health and what we eat from the day of birth throughout life: unsatisfactory nutritional habits can have undesirable and far-reaching effects. The foundations for later problems may be laid even before birth, though problems of intra-uterine growth retardation are of more concern in developing countries than in Western societies.

White identifies several reasons for the importance of nutritional education[5]:

1) It is necessary to equip the individual with the ability to make judicious food choices for health and well-being: good nutrition is vital to the achievement of genetic potential.
2) It allows the individual to evaluate the nutrition information he receives.
3) It promotes the best use of an individual's limited economic resources.
4) It reinforces knowledge and corrects faulty concepts about nutrition.
5) In global terms it helps to save money and avoid waste.

Nutrition education can be carried out in many different ways and at many different organisational levels. For example, Ritchie[6] sees that . . .'Nutritionists have as a first educational priority the task of impressing on governments the need for a food and nutrition policy to be included in their economic planning.'

Griffin and Light[7] illustrate this role of nutrition education at governmental level, in the formulating of policies; in agricultural and manufacturing industries, as shapers of food supply; and directly to the consumer.

Education in nutrition serves society in two ways. It acts as a conserving force maintaining the viability of the culture, and also as an innovative force facilitating adjustment to contemporary problems and conditions[7]. There is a tremendous gap between current nutrition knowledge and the dissemination and application of such knowledge. It is generally accepted that the state of nutrition knowledge and its application is poor amongst the general public. People do not

[5]White P. (1976) *Journal of Nutrition Education* 8, 2.
[6]Ritchie J.A.S. (1967) *Learning Better Nutrition*. FAO Nutritional Studies No. 20. FAO. Rome.
[7]Griffin G., Light, L. (1975) *Nutrition Education Curricula: relevance, design and the problem of change*. UNESCO Educational Studies and Documents. No. 18. Paris UNESCO.

instinctively choose what is best for them, and so nutrition education becomes an essential activity.

The effectiveness of nutrition education

In any programme designed to teach new material, evaluation should be an integral part of the scheme. The purpose of evaluation of nutrition programmes should be to determine whether they are effective in improving the overall standard of nutrition in the target group. The lack of such evaluation in many past nutrition programme is lamented . . . 'Teachers must constantly check the extent and clarity of the pupils knowledge obtained from specific lectures or units of instruction and any misunderstandings on their part must be corrected.'[8].

Turner suggests that frequent standard questionnaires should be presented to pupils to find out how much nutrition information they have taken in and thus assess the strengths and weaknesses of the programme. Assessment of the programme is an essential activity. Teachers must look dispassionately at their techniques, and try to encourage feedback from the pupils as to how they feel about the course, as well as how much they have remembered.[9]

One of the purposes of evaluation is ensuring that any new programme makes better use of the resources available than existing schemes.

A contrast can be made between the success of conventional didactic methods of teaching, and less formal participative methods. In the conventional method, facts are delivered to children in a formal manner, by the teacher, who remains at the front of the classroom. It is claimed that this approach is conducive to learning as the teacher is perceived as an authoritarian figure by the children, who are therefore more willing to accept the facts given to them. However, as Jelliffe (1970) says '. . . until recently, nutrition was taught in the old style of "do this because I tell you it is good" idiom, and so was neither suited to local conditions nor carried out in a manner which related to the community's existing beliefs'.[10]

Further, it has been suggested that this approach assumes a complete lack of knowledge of existing ideas about nutrition, and also that the children are merely waiting for the facts in order to act upon them.

Participative learning is more informal, where the child and the teacher work together to reinforce facts previously given. It is more practically orientated, pupils learning through tasks performed, and not being retricted to facts alone.

[8]Turner C.H. (1966) *Planning for Health Education in Schools*. Collins UNESCO.
[9]Briggs A. (1974) *Journal of the Royal Society of Health* 4, 155.
[10]Jelliffe D.B. (1968) *Child Nutrition in Developing Countries*. US Govt. Printing Office. Washington D.C.

Learning is a personal activity and it goes on all the time like breathing. Changes and improvements come about as a result of the learner's own efforts to understand, to make choices and decisions, and to do things differently. The desire to learn comes from within '. . . all concerned with health and nutrition education must understand the desires, purposes and interests of the people with whom they work.'[11] Jelliffe believes that it is the duty of the teacher to discover the interests of the children, and to adapt the approach accordingly, in order to stimulate and hold their attention. This could only be achieved by the method of participation and discussion.

Raw (1977) states that changing food habits is a main expectation of and challenge to nutrition education[12]. However '. . . there is no substantial evidence that this goal has ever been achieved.' Many studies belie this assertion.

Benson's early work in rural schools in the United States indicated that children improve their food practices when they:

1) discover for themselves what changes they have to make;
2) are strongly motivated to learn about foods and apply what they learn to their own diets; and
3) have access to the right kinds and amounts of food.[13]

Shortbridge[14] believes that learner success orientated education can achieve higher levels of learner success and stimulate learner motivation. This type of learning is based on three proven principles:

1) People learn best when supplied with relevant facts and information that they will use during the instruction. However, only the basic information necessary to acquire the skill should be given.
2) People learn best when given the opportunity to practice the skills which are to be learnt. The practice should be:
   a) appropriate to the subject
   b) frequent enough to ensure mastery
   c) permit individual performance
3) People learn faster when supplied with feedback on their progress.

Reasons for the apparent lack of success in nutrition teaching may include:
it is taught as a complicated science; over-simplification analogies are used; it is not backed up by appropriate practical work.[15]

Whitehead carried out an extensive literature search on nutrition education research, many studies dating from the 1940s.

This survey of nutrition education research showed that such work

[11]Clements F.W. (1955) *FAO Nutrition Meetings Report Series No. 13* FAO Rome.
[12]Raw I. (1977) *Proceedings of 1st Conference of Nutrition Education* In Press Oxford.
[13]Benson M.C. (1944) *Nutrition Education Series No. 5* Office of Education, Washington D.C.
[14]Shortbridge R. (1976) *Journal of Nutrition Education* 8, 1.
[15]Christian Carter J. (1975) *Housecraft*. August/September.

has been directed more toward disseminating nutrition information than improving dietary habits[16]. However, there is evidence that nutrition education which purports to improve dietary practices can be expected to do so within carefully defined limitations.

Frequently authors state that changing food habits is a complex process and requires long periods of time. The method used is probably more important than the length of time *per se*. Lewin, the pioneer of the discussion/decision method, suggests that in fact it may be possible to bring about in a relatively short time definite changes in food habits, even in food items which would be expected to show greater resistance to change. Age and interest level of the learner are as important as considerations of time.[17]

Whitehead draws the following broad conclusions from research in nutrition education . . .

1) Problem-solving is an effective way to influence what to do about their dietary intakes and their food supply. The challenge for nutrition educators is to create learning situations where people will recognise their own nutrition problems, then guide them step by step through the active process of problem-solving.
2) Discussion/decision is more effective than is admonition by lecture as a method of influencing what people do about dietary habits and nutrition problems.
   The discussion/decision method has been used successfully to stimulate people to try new foods, to select better ways of preparing foods and to make better food choices. The discussion/decision method may be a first step in certain situations to get people to recognise their own nutritional problems and to provide the stimulation needed to seek solutions to such problems.
3) Effective nutrition education, based on recognised needs, is co-operatively planned, conducted and evaluated, and supervised by adequately prepared nutrition educators. This implies that there is greater need for teachers to understand the fundamentals of nutrition.

The next chapter considers aspects of nutrition education at differing levels of implementation. Particular attention is given to the school, where many strategies are available.

---

[16]Whitehead F.E. (1975) *World Review of Nutrition and Dietetics* 17, 91.
[17]Lewin K. (1943) *National Research Council Bill* 108 Washington DC.

12: Nutrition education in the school

'Nutrition Education is a learning process, its overall aim being to improve the nutritional status and health of the learner'. [1]

Authorities are agreed that the teaching of nutritional facts should be seen only as a necessary step in influencing food habits and not as an end in itself. In nutrition, predominantly, it is practice rather than knowledge which is important. Any form of relevant education should give the pupil some general ideas which would stimulate and guide his own development rather than lead to a well-informed individual [2].

Ritchie [3] lists five general aims of nutrition education in schools:

1) 'To promote good health and development in schoolchildren'.

Health is of prime importance to man, and good health cannot be achieved without good nutrition. 'Nutrition may be the most important aspect of learning to the well-being of future generations and the ability of human groups to survive in future.' [4]

2) 'To establish good food practices'.

What is defined as 'good food practice' will vary between different cultures and with different circumstances. It is important to study existing knowledge of, and attitudes to, food and eating and to observe current practice as a precursor to effecting changes in food habits.

3) 'To develop healthy attitudes to food and enjoyment of well-prepared, nutritious meals'.

Emphasis should be put on the importance of developing attitudes which will favour desirable food practices. It is well accepted that a positive attitude towards an action is a necessary, though not sufficient, precursor to carrying out that action.

4) 'To teach them the principles of good nutrition and the importance and application of these in daily life'.

Christian describes how the child must learn necessary scientific concepts before being able to appreciate the relationship of food to health [5]. The lack of success in much nutrition teaching may be because

[1] Burton P. (1966) *Nutricion Humana* Washington DC.
[2] Whitehead A.N. (1961) *Los Fines de la Education*. Buenos Aires. Paidos.
[3] Ritchie J.A.S. (1967) *Learning Better Nutrition*. FAO Nutritional Studies. No. 20. FAO. Rome.
[4] Griffin G., Light L. (1975) *Nutrition Education Curricula*. UNESCO Educational Studies and Documents No. 18.
[5] Christian-Carter J. (1978) *Nutrition and Food Science* 54.

the children acquire 'empty facts' without understanding fundamentals. The Food and Agricultural Organisation expect, perhaps rather naively, that 'middle class families of Europe and America have been brought up to respect science and value its results'!

'Once the facts have been presented to them, these families tend to accept new food or a new concept about food and its relationship to health.'

'Thus education, and particularly science education will aid the application of new scientific knowledge to the improvement of the diet.'[6]

This view does not seem to take account of the various models of health behaviour, and it is even more doubtful whether it would apply to under-privileged non-middle class children.

5) 'To help them (children) acquire skills in the production, storage, selection, preservation and preparation of food, which will assist them in obtaining a good diet'.

Ritchie was writing primarily with developing countries in mind, where the the child probably has more responsibility for his own food intake. It is equally applicable however, to Western youngsters who will, as homemakers, require the above skills to feed their families. Thus the learning of skills is essential if theory is to be translated into practice. The child should leave school with something that he knows well and something which he can do well. A little good information is better than a mass of irrelevancies.

The Schools Council Project: *Health Education 5-13*[7] says of its nutrition component 'this unit is intended to help children understand the importance of food to their lives, and more particularly to their health, happiness and growth'. These general aims have widespread validity, but the specific objectives of any particular nutrition programme will depend upon local needs and environment.

Rationale

Ritchie sums up the rationale for nutrition education in school as follows:

a) Children are not set in their ways.
b) They are more open-minded and used to accepting new ideas as a part of growing up.
c) They have great curiosity, have wide interests and are eager to learn.
d) They are subject to peer group pressures.
e) They form a useful bridge in approaching families.
f) They will be future parents.
g) They form a captive audience.

Because nutrition is a living subject which affects an individual every

[6]FAO (1962) *FFHC Basic Study No. 6* FAO Rome.
[7]Schools Council (1977) *Health Education 5-13 yr.* Nelson. London.

day of his life and can influence his future well-being, it is desirable that nutrition education starts as soon after the child is born as possible. This in turn implies that attitudes and behaviours of the parents should be conducive to the child acquiring good food habits as part of the primary socialisation process. During the early years at school, the child's ideas, including those concerning food and dietary habits, are still in a formative stage and are more readily influenced than are those of an adult.

As the child gets older, dietary habits become more engrained and more resistant to change. Children aged 5 to 14 years are *more* open-minded and are likely to be receptive to changes in ideas and agreeable to modifications of eating habits. They are also used to accepting new knowledge and ideas as part of growing up, and new ideas fit into the concept of the school being a place of change.

Group pressures also play a part. The desire to imitate others or even excel them in their nutritional experiences contributes greatly to the change in habits and attitudes of pupils[8]. A person's behaviour is influenced by other people inasmuch as he derives satisfaction or disappointment by comparing his lot with theirs and, before making a decision, considers what they would do in the circumstances or what they will think of him because of his choice. The people he uses for comparison are for him a 'reference group'. A reference group of a person's peers may be potent in guiding his behaviour becauses he wishes to be accepted and approved by the rest of the members. This usually means conforming to their ways and standards because deviation from the expected behaviour of the group is likely to arouse hostility. The wish to conform can have desirable or undesirable effects in a nutrition programme. It can make it difficult to break with tradition and try something new, or, if the majority are already in favour, it can help to bring dissenting members into line with others.

Often people are ignorant of basic rules of diet, and this is observed in all socio-economic classes and in all societies[9]. The establishment of a formal home-school link might allow the child to become an agent of change, correcting erroneous beliefs and transmitting reliable information.

It should not be overlooked that the children of the present will be the parents of the future, and will pass on to their children their own dietary norms. The cycle must be entered somewhere and the school would seem to be an appropriate place to do this. A further advantage in this country is that the vast majority of children do pass through the educational system. Thus problems of accessibility are solved.

[8] Martin D.A. (1963) *Nutrition Education in Action – A Guide for teachers.* Holt, Rinehart and Winston.
[9] Wilson H.R., Lamb M.W. (1968) *Journal of Home Economics* 60, 2.

It has frequently been pointed out that the teaching of nutrition in schools may not only be unsuccessful in changing food habits established during primary socialisation, but may also create emotional and psychological conflicts in the child who finds a disparity between what his teachers say and what his parents say, or what actually happens in the home environment. Alternatively, the child may reject what is taught at school, or may comply whilst at school but re-adopt family values at home. This problem of 'culture clash' is particularly apparent in nutrition with immigrant children and to a lesser extent with children from the lower socio-economic classes. However, Bavly found that one of the major factors affecting changes in adult eating behaviour was the influence of children returning home from school having learnt about nutrition and eaten the foods served there for lunch[10]. Thomas commented that a mutuality of influence occurs which cannot be ignored, though unless gains won in the classroom are mirrored and supported in the community at large, there is a danger that behaviour potentiality will give way to habitual practices[11].

Context

'It is difficult to say with certainty what importance is imputable to health education, since in a general sense, it is not merely a subject that the child must learn, but is also a continuous educative process developed by means of the whole series of subjects studied and activities carried out at school'.[12]

There are many possible ways of introducing nutrition into the school curriculum and each has its supporters in the literature. It is likely that in practice, circumstances will largely dictate what methods are feasible.

There are two main lines of thought as to the form nutrition education should take:

1) Nutrition taught as a formal school subject with an allocated number of hours in the curriculum.
2) Nutrition is integrated into existing curriculum subject areas.

It has been claimed that granting separate status to nutrition increases its importance in the eyes of the pupil[13].

On the other hand 'Nutrition teaching should be a permanent and continual process with a specific well-planned methodology; it cannot be relegated to one or two hours per week.'[14]

Integration of food and nutrition education with all school subjects, whether obviously related or not, is the best way of converting the

[10]Bavly S. (1964) *Food Habits and their Change in Israel:* College of Nutrition and Home Economics: Ministry of Education and Culture Jerusalem.
[11]Thomas J.E. (1979) *Journal of the Royal Society of Health* 5.
[12]UNESCO (1967) *IBE Publication No. 304* UNESCO Paris.
[13]Holmes, M. (1970) *School Science Review*. July.
[14]F.A.O. (1971) *FAO Nutritional Studies No. 25*. FAO. Rome.

educative act into a permanent action which favours achievement of the final objective – change of attitudes and habits. Continuous reinforcement is harmonious with the fact that nutrition education is a continuous process.

The topics that need to be covered for children to have an all-round knowledge of nutrition are too diverse to be taught as one subject. It would be easier for the teachers involved, and also would give the children new angles on the subject, to teach nutrition through various timetabled subjects.[15].

Nutrition could be taught in biology, art and craft, home economics, science and general courses. It is not difficult to introduce nutrition into any subject on the timetable. A total programme of work needs to be planned and structured to include all the necessary topics.

The Schools Council bulletin also makes allusions to the hidden curriculum. For nutrition this includes school meals and tuck shops, as well as personal example: *'Every effort should be made by teachers at all stages of education to develop the link with the school catering officer and to recognise fully the potential value of the school meals service as an educational resource'.*[16].

However, school meals as part of the hidden curriculum may not form a sound basis for nutrition teaching, as proper preparation and cooking cannot be relied on. Children should be given an understanding not only of the nutritional value of the school meal but also of the reasons why it is provided. If the meal provided is well cooked and consumed in a pleasant environment it could form a useful addition to classroom teaching. Too often, meals are cooked in a central kitchen and delivered to individual schools, resulting in deterioration of nutritional value and general quality, and consequently do not provide a 'good example'.

Referring to tuck shops, the Schools Council suggest that these could be used as a vehicle for promoting sound food selection.

'Whereas they may provide a worthy profit margin to strengthen school funds, they generally fail to support the development of responsible attitudes towards sound health.'

It would not be too difficult to replace the typical cariogenic offerings with more nutritious alternatives.

[15]Morant R.W. (1971) *Health Educational Journal* 29, 2.
[16]Schools Council (1971) *Occasional Bulletin: Approaches to Nutrition Education.*

13: Communication of innovations

Communication of innovations is concerned with social change, and it offers a theoretical explanation of why a projected change may be adopted or rejected, by examining the nature and characteristics of the elements involved. It aids an appreciation of the difficulties facing a change-agent, and has obvious implications for the educator concerned with promoting changes in health behaviour.

Change may occur through forces acting within the social system, when it is termed 'immanent', or may be derived from external sources – 'contact' – in which case it is either selective or directed. Directed contact change is brought about by outsiders who deliberately seek to introduce new ideas to achieve defined goals. The health educator is frequently concerned with planned or directed change.

Communication of innovation is specifically concerned with the spread of messages that lead to *new* practices being adopted. The consequences of accepting or rejecting an innovation often involve an element of risk and this has certain implications for projected behaviour changes.

In normal human social interaction most communication takes place between individuals who share certain attributes such as similar beliefs and values, or education and social status. This phenomenon is termed homophily, and it seems that most people, given the choice, select homophilous receivers for their communications. In this situation the effectiveness of communication is likely to be improved, as problems of social distance and incompatible values are minimised. In communications of innovations it is almost axiomatic that there will exist between the sender and the receiver some degree of heterophily. That is, knowledge, beliefs and and values will differ. If that were not the case, the sender would hardly be in a position to act as an innovator. The extent of sender-receiver heterophily leads to special problems in securing effective communication. Social distance and transcultural barriers will increase heterophily and thus the difficulty of communication.

The main elements in the diffusion of new ideas are:
1) **The innovation**.
2) Which is **communicated** through certain **channels**.
3) Over **time**.
4) Among the **members of a social system**.

An **innovation** is an idea, practice or object perceived as being new by an individual and the characteristics of the innovation, as perceived, determine its rate of adoption. Five such characteristics of innovations are:

1) Relative advantage
2) Compatability
3) Complexity
4) Trialability
5) Observability

The greater the perceived *relative advantage* of an innovation, the more rapid its rate of adoption. This coincides with value expectancy theory, which says that an action must be seen to have more advantages before it is endorsed. This may be in the form of practical gains or losses for self and significant others, and as approval as opposed to disapproval of self and others.

Compatability is the degree to which an innovation is perceived as being consistent with the existing values, past experiences, and needs of the receivers. An idea that is incompatible with the prevalent values and norms of the social system will not be adopted as swiftly as an innovation which is compatible. The adoption of an incompatible innovation requires the prior adoption of a new value system. In the field of nutritional health many examples of incompatibility can be cited, eg the promotion of meat as a good protein food in school classes with Hindu children; the advocacy of margarine as a source of vitamin D for immigrants; the promotion of citrus fruit to the elderly – many of whom believe these foods are acid and will harm them.

Complexity is the degree to which an innovation is perceived as being difficult to understand and use. Those innovations which require little effort from the receiver will be adopted more rapidly than those demanding new skills and understanding. Effort required and perceived gains can be considered together. A simple representation of their relationship is shown in *Figure 13.1*, indicating symbolically expected results.

Trialability is the degree to which an innovation may be experimented with on a limited basis. New ideas which can be tried out temporarily or partly will generally be adopted more quickly than innovations which are not divisible. A trialable innovation represents less risk to the individual who is considering it, eg substituting saccharin for sugar is eminently trialable, whilst fluoridation is not.

Observability is the degree to which the results of an innovation are visible to others. The easier it is for an individual to see the results of an innovation, the more likely he is to adopt it. Many 'desirable' health behaviours do not have observable effects because they are in essence preventive actions, eg it is not possible to directly observe the effects of diet in preventing coronary heart disease (if they exist).

Having defined the major attributes of an innovation it is obvious that

99

if the message is to be spread, communication must take place. Variables associated with the communication process have been described elsewhere[1], but essentially are concerned with the source, message and receiver. The message is transmitted via a communication **channel**. The choice of channel usually depends on the purpose of the message and the nature of the receiver: this choice may be important in determining whether an innovation is adopted or rejected.

Figure 13.1 Effort vs Gains

Effort

		HIGH	LOW
Gains	HIGH	INTER	GOOD
	LOW	POOR	INTER

Contrast avoidance of fried foods for patient with painful ulcer, with avoidance of sweets by normal child.

Communication channels can be classified as either:

    a) Interpersonal   or mass media
    b) Local   or cosmopolitan

These channels play different roles in creating knowledge or in persuading individuals to change their attitudes towards innovations and may often be combined to advantage.

Mass media channels are all those means of transmitting messages that involve a mass-medium, and thus enable one individual to reach a large audience quickly. Interpersonal channels are those that involve a face-to-face exchange between two or more individuals. Mass media channels are relatively more important at creating knowledge and spreading information, whilst interpersonal channels are more effective in persuading, or changing attitudes. Interpersonal channels have the advantage of allowing a two-way exchange of ideas. The receiver is thus able to obtain clarification or additional information about the innovation from the source individual. Problems of selective exposure perception and retention may thus be decreased. This suggests that mass media could be effectively used for disseminating health knowledge, but would not be particularly effective in bringing about change in attitude or behaviour. To accomplish the latter, interpersonal channels must be utilised.

Mass media channels are almost exclusively cosmopolite as they are outside the social system. Other sources of new ideas originate within the

[1]Lennon D., Fieldhouse P. (1980) *Community Dietetics* Forbes London.

social system and are referred to as localite. Cosmopolite channels are relatively more important at imparting knowledge, and localite channels are relatively more important in the persuasion function. These two dimensions: mass media – interpersonal and cosmopolite – localite are distinct though related. Mass media and cosmopolite channels have their greatest effect on early adopters (those individuals who first adopt the innovation) as they are external sources of new ideas. The early adopters then act as localite, interpersonal channels for the later-adopters. This suggests that early adopters are more 'change-orientated' and require less active persuasion to change.

Mass media and interpersonal channels can often be combined to advantage. 'Media forums' are organised small groups of individuals who meet regularly to receive a mass media programme, and to discuss its contents. They appear to be successful because they exert social pressure on attendance and participation and because attitude change is more readily achieved when individuals are in groups.

(Lewin[2] illustrates the uses of group discussion/decision in promoting advantageous nutritional practices.)

This consideration of communication channels is of direct relevance to the nutritional educator. It demonstrates that methods need to be chosen to suit purposes and that a combination of techniques is probably most desirable.

The next element of the process of innovation to consider is **time**. A considerable time-lag may occur between exposure to a new idea and its ultimate rejection or acceptance. The rate of adoption will vary in different circumstances and individuals may be categorised according to the speed with which they adopt an innovation. Rogers and Shoemaker[3] identify four stages in the adoption/rejection of an innovation:

1) Knowledge
2) Persuasion
3) Decisions
4) Confirmation

These stages are reminiscent of the stages in health action models. The relative time at which an innovation is adopted allows classification of adopters as:

1) Innovators
2) Early adopters
3) Early majority
4) Late majority
5) Laggards

The rate of adoption of an innovation by a social group is usually measured by the length of time required for a certain percentage of the

[2]Lewin K. (1942) *Committee on Food Habits* National Research Council Washington DC.
[3]Rogers E.M., Shoemaker F. (1971) *Communication of Innovations* United States of America, Free Press.

group to adopt the innovations. Social systems typified by modern, rather than traditional norms will have a faster rate of adoption.

A **social system** with modern norms is more change-orientated, technologically developed, scientific, rational, cosmopolite and empathic. (Rogers and Shoemaker p.33). This suggests that within the United Kingdom, say, higher social status groups would accept innovations more rapidly than low groups, eg cessation of smoking and frequency of breast feeding are higher in social groups I and II.

An important concept in communication of innovations theory is that of opinion leadership. In any social group, certain members function as opinon leaders. They provide information and advice about innovation to many others in the system. These leaders usually enjoy high social status, are more cosmopolite and are more exposed to external communications: they are able to influence other peoples attitudes or behaviour with relative frequency, not through any formal authority or power, but because of their social respectability. Opinion leaders are usually members of the social system in which they exert their influence and are very useful contacts for the external agent seeking to bring about a desired change within the system. (cf – the use of disc-jockeys and footballers in safety campaigns).

Innovation decisions may be:
> 1) optional – made by an individual regardless of others
> 2) collective – a consensus decision of a social group
> 3) authoritative – dictated by a 'governing' body

Examples of these within the health field are:
> a) smoking
> b) fluoridation
> c) crash helmets

Authoritative decisions are adopted most quickly, perhaps through fear of sanctions for non-compliance, though they may be circumvented as discontinued with time – Festinger (1971)[4] points out that forced compliance is frequently followed by a change of personal attitudes in an attempt to reduce cognitive dissonance.

Individual or optional decisions are adopted more quickly than collective ones. Health education is usually most concerned with optional decisions – though some lobbies would press for more authoritative control.

Community development depends upon the acceptance of change. Communication of innovations theory provides a description of the processes occurring in a community when a change is proposed or a new idea introduced. It may be useful in predicting the barriers likely to be encountered when a new idea is introduced and this helps in the design and implementation of programmes. For example, knowledge of

[4]Festinger L. (1971) *A Theory of Cognitive Dissonance* Stamford University Press.

population characteristics helps to define the type of social system and its likely change orientation. Methods can be selected on the basis of knowledge of the relative effectiveness of mass-media and interpersonal communications and opinion leaders can be identified and 'recruited'.

Appropriate strategies can thus be identified, to maximise the chances of successful change.

14: Nutrition in higher education

Apart from those specifically studying nutritional subjects, there are a number of groups whose education does or could include some nutritional input. The amount and type of nutrition taught will be dependent on a number of factors, including professional needs, subject priorities and time-availability.

Professional needs relate to what kind of involvement the qualified student will have with nutrition education. It may be a direct teaching position, an advisory role, or an occasional encounter with nutritional problems. The content of courses should reflect these needs, so that the knowledge and skills taught are seen to be relevant. Time-availability and subject priorities often go together in a crowded timetable. Nutrition may be just one more subject, competing with a host of other specialities: this reason is often advanced for the current lack of nutritional teaching in medical schools. Ample evidence has been accumulated to suggest that better nutrition has been a major contributor to improvements in community health: its importance is unlikely to decrease. For this reason alone it is desirable that all community health workers have some acquaintance with nutritional principles.

As nutritional issues receive more attention in lay circles, the demand for information from professional sources is likely to increase. Health care workers should be at least superficially familiar with current nutrition theories – especially where practical advice is likely to be needed, eg infant feeding, ischaemic heart disease, the fibre controversy.

In the following sections the current position of nutrition in the higher education sectors is reviewed.

Nutrition and dietetics

There are a number of courses available at undergraduate and postgraduate level, which offer specific training in Nutrition and Dietetics. Undergraduate courses are normally of three or four years duration, and lead to a degree qualification: they may include periods of clinical dietetic training, in which case State Registration in Dietetics is also available.

The content of the various courses available differs from institution to institution and varying emphasis is placed on sections within the courses. Common to them all is the study of nutritional theory, usually backed by a considerable amount of biochemical and physiological science. Other sciences usually include microbiology and mathematics or statistics. Food science and technology may be a minor or major component. Dietetics is obviously a central subject, except where it is offered as an option or addition. Food studies and catering generally come into the picture and sometimes the amount of time devoted to these subjects is disproportionately high.

An essential component of nutrition and dietetics courses can be termed behavioural science. This includes aspects of sociology and psychology which are pertinent to health care: it helps to provide a broader perspective on nutritional problems and emphasises the people orientation of dietetics. Guidelines for courses have been recently prepared by the Dietetics Board[1].

It is perhaps unfortunate that students entering such courses are required to have solely scientific qualifications. The rationale for this is not entirely clear. Whilst a knowledge of basic science is clearly advantageous in approaching such subjects as biochemistry and physiology, it is of limited value as a preparation for social studies. Indeed, students steeped in 'the scientific method' may find it harder to come to terms with methods of social investigation. Another 'advantage' of the prerequisite for science is that a more homogenous group of students is selected, which helps to minimise some of the potential problems of teaching a subject to students with different backgrounds.

Of course, analogous problems would arise if only social science background students were accepted. Traditionally, nutrition has been seen as a scientific subject, which may partly explain its prerequirements. Unfortunately, scientific study is not always encouraged, or available to female school pupils, and as dietetics especially, is still a female-orientated profession, many candidates are rejected on grounds of inappropriate subject choices. Additionally, until recently, 'A' level qualifications in social sciences were not readily available. As awareness of nutrition as a social science as well as a scientific one increases, there should hopefully be some attempt to achieve more adaptability in entrance requirements.

Structuring of academic courses could also be modified to accommodate a more flexible approach. First-year remedial courses could be offered to overcome the worst effects of a heterogenous intake, whilst more scope for specialisation or options could be incorporated in later years. Close guidance of student choices would be necessary to maintain an integral course, and more emphasis is put on individual skills and attainment rather than a 'mass product'. In addition, there would need to be closer definition of what is 'essential' what is 'desirable' and what is 'peripheral'.

[1]Dietitians Board (1980) *Guidelines for 4-year courses in Dietetics.*

Figure 14.1 Illustrates schematically typical existing course patterns (a) and a possible alternative (b).

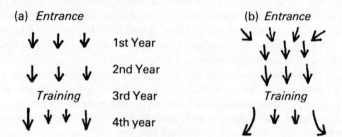

Medical studies

Nutrition as part of the curricula of medical schools is generally not well developed[2]. What little is included usually appears in biochemistry and physiology courses and concerns nutritional theory rather than application. In view of the undoubted role of the diet in many of the common disorders seen by the doctor, it is important that he should be at least familiar with nutritional topics. Of course, we don't suggest that the doctor should be a master of nutritional theory – there are other specialists who fulfil this function – but he should be in a position to give basic advice and to know when consultation with a nutrition professional would be advantageous. Nutrition in medical schools could be taught by a visiting dietitian or nutritionist, though preferably there would be a nutritionist on the staff.

Health visitors

Health visitors are prime contacts for the nutrition educator, as they are in a position to disseminate knowledge and especially on nutritional matters, amongst certain groups of the population. It is obvious that the health visitor, a field worker, should be in a position to give accurate and up-to-date nutritional advice. A series of lectures or workshops on nutrition should certainly be included in any training programme, and the most suitable content can be determined by consultation between nutritionist and health visitor tutor. As in courses for other health professionals, the role and skills of dietitian or other nutrition educator should be made clear.

Nurses

Nurses are another group who have direct communication with clients. In hospitals they often have the responsibility for the final stage of food

[2]Fieldhouse P., de Looy A.E. (1978) *Proceedings of the Nutrition Society* 37, 35a.

provision to the patient, and are also in the front line for answering patients questions on all medical and paramedical matters. The district nurse and midwife, working in the community have a similar omnipotent role – and also have the opportunity to promote positive nutritional messages.

Nursing courses should contain an element of nutrition – awareness of the importance of diet in care of the patient. More specific in-service courses can be offered to all these groups as appropriate, and individuals with particular interests in nutrition should be encouraged to develop their skills in this area, but nurse tutors must be encouraged to use nutritionists and dietitians to provide the input of nutrition education so that relevant up-to-date material is taught.

Teachers

If nutrition education in schools is accepted as being a valuable pursuit, then it is obvious that teachers must be willing and able to explore this topic. Although it would be unreasonable to expect teachers to become subject experts, they could receive some realistic guidance. In teacher training courses those could be:

1) A general compulsory course on health education – this would briefly survey major issues, but would concentrate on rationale and methodology of teaching.
2) A more specialised option on nutrition education – again context and methodology would be covered and in addition resources and activities could be dealt with.

As with the various health-professionals, teachers might benefit from in-service courses dealing with different aspects of nutrition, and at different levels. The nutrition educator must work through groups such as these – and be willing to assist and encourage – and in the end, trust others.

A range of other courses concerned with health and social care could usefully have a nutritional input. This might take the form of one or two sessions given by a visiting nutritonist – where the aim is as always to promote awareness of the importance of nutrition to health, and the need for it to be considered in both treatment and in policy decisions. Groups who might benefit from such an input include social workers, health administrators, and planners, probation officers, nursery nurses, and catering administrators, both in the NHS and more importantly in industry.

Nutrition is a vast topic, and is not the province of one type of professional. The nutrition educator must be seen as a co-ordinator and resource specialist, who is willing to allow others to take on nutritional responsibilities – and ensure that they are capable of doing so. However, he or she should endeavour never to lose touch with field work – for this leads to loss of touch with reality.

107

15:Community education

As previously discussed, the family unit is the main influence on the primary socialisation process. It provides the social and physical environment in which eating takes place, and to a large extent governs the food habits of its members, by controlling availability. Ideally, the child will be provided with models of good eating practices, so that later education will have a sound base to build on. The child entering school already has developed eating patterns and attitudes to food, and education at this level must accommodate these. Because of the strong influence of the family, they form a good target for the nutrition educator.

Disparities often arise between what is taught in the home and what is taught at school: it would be unrealistic to expect that school-learning is often filtered back into the home, bringing about a change of practices there. Therefore, a more direct approach may be more productive. There are opportunities, however, to develop home-school links, through extra-mural activities, and by encouraging parents to visit schools and participate in some aspects of school work.

Accessibility to the family unit is limited, and there may be little opportunity for direct contact. Adult education classes, for example, concerned with cookery or with health care, may attract some people: however, this implies existing motivation and concern and may not be equally attractive to all socio-economic groups. Work with individual families may be accomplished through other professionals – such as the health visitor or social worker. Such people regularly visit homes and are in a position to identify problem areas, and to supply information and advice on health matters.

Obviously, a close working relationship is needed between the nutrition educator and these professionals, if such advice is to be practical and up-to-date. Possibly the nutrition educator could undertake domiciliary visits – perhaps initially on a referral basis. In most instances though, the concern will be with nutrition problems that arise, or with at-risk individuals and families. The scope for positive promotion of good nutrition is more limited.

Another approach would be to utilise normative influences which effect the food habits of the family by looking at local availability and acceptability of foodstuffs, or by utilising mass media channels. It is extremely difficult for the individual worker to make much impact on availability: requests to local bakeries and supermarkets to make wholemeal and wheatmeal bread available are likely to meet with mixed success! A local project involving price manipulation was greeted with enthusiasm, though no evaluative data is available: some local supermarkets were persuaded to put certain foods on special offer – whilst a leaflet campaign was running which was aimed at promoting the use of whole cereals, fruit and vegetable.

Mass media channels

The use of mass media channels is one possible way of presenting nutrition messages to the general public. Problems of selective exposure occur and it is likely that messages will be ineffective for audiences who are not previously motivated. Communication of innovations theory suggests that whilst mass media channels may successfully impart information, they are unlikely to have any persuasive effect. Provision of information is, however, a useful and often essential precursor to attitude or behaviour change.

Television

The enterprising nutrition educator may find a number of ways of using TV presentations to impart sound nutritional advice. Because the television is a pervasive medium, audiences will be large, and the opportunities for giving simple messages should be fully exploited. Short interviews on news magazine programmes will have popular appeal, when both basic advice and discussion of contemporary issues can be covered eg provision of school lunches. Regular comment on 'hot' nutritonal concerns is another possibility.

More ambitious projects may include contributing to documentary programmes or features. Programmes especially for schools could offer opportunities, and there have recently been several series which deal with aspects of health.

Despite the disadvantages associated with indirect communication, the television does have an (perhaps undeservedly) air of credibility. In addition to the actual content of a broadcast, the presentation can be useful as a way of informing people of the existence of the nutrition educator, and of any nutritional services available.

Radio

Radio is probably more accessible as a medium although it lacks the visual impact of television. Local radio stations in particular are usually happy to give air-time to anyone with something worth saying! Phone-ins are still very popular, and those concerned with nutrition or health, especially so. Again, although the educational content of such programmes is limited, awareness of nutritional services can be promoted.

National radio has, in the last year or so, broadcast a number of series which have been concerned with food and nutrition. Although these have in the main been well presented and interesting, they have generally been conceived by professional communicators – not professional nutritionists. A marriage of interests is obviously necessary here.

Press

Newspapers and magazines form the third mass outlet and have a very wide readership. Many magazines – particularly those aimed primarily at women – carry features on nutrition, and very rarely are these written by a qualified nutritionist. Morever, the magazines tend to be 'up-market' and food presentation is the major concern, rather than nutritional value. Social norms can also be communicated: for example, certain types of foods may be promoted either intentionally or not, by being associated with 'desirable' lifestyles. There is certainly tremendous scope here for the nutrition educator with literary abilities. Information presented in magazines is probably more acceptable than if presented in the form of leaflets emanating from a professional source.

Newspapers are widely read, and there are many different styles to suit (audience) needs. Local newspapers may have advantages in being acceptable and credible – an organ of the community.

Regular features, question and answer columns, topical comments and recipe pages all offer possibilities for providing sound nutritional information.

Using mass-media channels helps to solve a major problem in community education – that of access. Simply getting audience and educators together is a major problem – although personal contact is eminently desirable if attempts are being made to actually change food habits.

Personal contact may be possible through some of the organisations listed below:

Ante-natal classes	Factories
Pre-school groups	Adult education classes
School	Residential homes and day
Young wives groups	care centres – a) elderly,
Women's Institute	b) handicapped
Church groups	Slimming groups
Youth clubs	Breast-feeding groups
Parent-teacher associations	Family service units

The authors were successful in establishing contacts with many of these types of organisation by offering 'nutrition talks' via the local radio station. The response was overwhelming, and provided opportunities for dietetic students to become involved in community nutrition education[1].

[1]Fieldhouse P. (1980) *Nutrition and Food Science*. 64.

Liaison with other professionals is also useful in creating opportunities for nutrition education. Social workers and health visitors particularly, have freer access to the general population.

The nutrition educator has a number of responsibilities as far as fellow professionals are concerned. These include acting as a resource for reliable nutrition information – which implies keeping an up-to-date review of the literature – assessing nutritional literature (leaflets etc) and recommending their selective use, and assisting in or involving others with community health programmes. Additionally lectures could be given on current nutritional issues, or, if the demand exists, full study days or even in-service courses. There is some indication that GPs, for example, would welcome many of the above mentioned 'support services'[2].

Another type of community service which could be initiated involves nutritional counselling, where members of the local population would have free access to general advice on any aspect of diet and nutrition – excepting, of course, therapeutic treatment. Procedures for setting up this kind of service would need to be carefully elucidated and frequent evaluation would be essential. The American Dietetic Association offer some useful guidelines[3]. The scale on which this kind of service could be offered depends on resources available: it could take the form of an information bureau for personal callers only, or might provide a phone-in service. Dial-a-Dietitian schemes operate successfully in many parts of North America[4], where community nutrition services are more accepted and developed than in the United Kingdom.

Finally, local nutritional groups could consider the production of a regular community newsheet – perhaps similar in format to those produced by Community Health Councils. To be at all effective, nutrition educators must first of all make themselves known in the community – by a concerted PR effort directed at media sources, fellow professionals, and community groups. Next, they must be willing to become involved in educational work, and not be content to sit behind an office desk.

[2]Fieldhouse P., de Looy A.E. (1978) *Proceedings of the Nutrition Society* 37, 5a.
[3]American Dietetic Association (1968) *Journal of the American Dietetic Association* 55, 4, p343.
[4]Wagner M.G. et al (1965) *Journal of the American Dietetic Association* 47, 5, p381.

Appendix

Sources of nutrition education and information

There are in the United Kingdom various organisations which seek to influence the nutrition or nutritional knowledge of the public. Some are specifically set up to sponsor research into nutrition and publish booklets and articles on nutrition. Others give out nutritional information as a sideline to the production of food, and a few food firms actually sponsor research. Then there are the professional bodies for those professionals concerned with nutrition. The following is a brief outline of the larger and more influencial organisations:

NATIONAL BODIES

Department of Health and Social Security

The DHSS sponsors research on nutrition and farms out surveillance field work to other bodies. It also sets up panels to make reports on current issues of nutritional importance, there have been many of these. The panels and subsequent reports are usually initiated in response to concern about the nutritional status of a section of the population or concern about a certain facet of nutrition.

The *Health Education Council* was set up in 1968 by the Secretary of State for Health and Social Services: it is a registered charity. Its brief is to advise on priorities for health education, to advise and carry out national, local and regional campaigns, the latter in co-operation with regional and area health authorities. It can also undertake or sponsor research, and acts as a national centre of expertise and knowledge in all aspects of health education. The Health Education Council also acts to encourage and promote training in health education. The Council produces numerous leaflets, including some on nutrition. The *Health Education Journal* comes out quarterly and there is also a monthly news sheet entitled *Health Education News*.

British Nutrition Foundation

This body describes its aims as promoting education and research in nutrition and related matters and providing information about nutrition in all its aspects. It has published several reports in conjunction with the British Dietetic Association, and a report on Nutrition Education in 1977. The *British Nutrition Foundation Bulletin* is brought out quarterly.

Nutrition Society

The Nutrition Society aims to advance the scientific study of nutrition and its application to the maintenance of human and animal health. The society holds meetings throughout the year at which papers are read, these are published in the *Proceedings of the Nutrition Society*, the society also.

publishes the *British Journal of Nutrition*. Membership is by election, and aspiring members must be proposed and seconded by members of the Nutrition Society.

PROFESSIONAL BODIES

These associations exist to encourage exchange of views within professions, thereby hopefully leading to a dynamic profession seeking after new truths. Statements giving the views of a profession may in fact be put out by these bodies on an issue where some strong professional comment is called for.

British Dietetic Association

This was established in 1936, it acts as an association for dietitians, and not only encourages and participates in the exchange of views in the profession, but also advises on training and produces leaflets for prospective students. It holds two conferences annually and branch meetings are held throughout the country. A magazine entitled *Nutrition* is brought out every two months. The association published *Wise Eating – a guide for the over 60s* in conjunction with the British Nutrition Foundation.

Institute of Health Education

The Institute exists for exchange of views and membership of all those interested in health education. It has a special section for professional educators. It holds conferences and meetings and publishes a journal quarterly; and a news letter every two months, which is free to members.

SELF-HELP BODIES

These societies are set up to promote contact for people suffering from certain chronic diseases. They also promote information on a variety of subjects including lists of special foods, and allowances available to patients; they are usually counselled by professionals in relevant fields. Some of the bigger organisations sponsor research.

We have not included the slimming organisations in this group as they do not fall into this category being commercial concerns.

British Diabetic Association

This association was founded in 1934, its aims are the provision of advisory and welfare services for diabetics. The association has a membership of 62,000 in the United Kingdom and is probably the biggest of its kind. It sponsors research and provides welfare services such as summer camps for diabetic children. A newspaper entitled *Balance* is published six times a year and numerous booklets on diet, carbohydrate exchanges and insulins, health care and information about special allowances are produced.

The Coeliac Society

This was formed in June 1968 to help children and adults who have coeliac disease. The society publishes lists of gluten free foods. The lists, which are constantly reviewed, are available to dietitians, doctors and other health care professionals as well as patients. A handbook is published by the association, and includes recipes and advice.

PKU Society
This society is for the parents of children suffering from phenylketonuria. The society publishes newsletters which contain recipes and medical news, and also holds meetings both regional and national.

MANUFACTURERS

Some food firms put out nutritional information on their products, this was initially as a service to dietitians and doctors, who often required to know what was in certain products. The large American companies were the first in the field to produce comprehensive food analysis charts of their products, but now most of the large British companies do also. Birds Eye have for the last few years employed a nutritionist to both give out information and answer queries about nutrition. Recently, Birds Eye have also started putting nutritional information onto labels, an innovation which may soon become obligatory for other food firms.

Van den Berghs, as well as providing information on their products, also sponsor a symposium entitled *Getting the most out of Food* which is held annually and the proceedings are published in a booklet. A prize is offered for the best essay.

Many manufacturers now use nutrition to try to sell their foods, but it may be that more stringent legislation is needed.

Index